D103 SOCIETY AND SOCIAL SCIENCE: A FOUNDATION COURSE

BLOCK 3
WORK, MARKETS AND THE ECONOMY

THE OPEN UNIVERSITY

D103 PRODUCTION TEAM

John Allen
James Anderson (Chairperson)
Robert Bocock
Peter Bradshaw
Vivienne Brown
Linda Clark (Course Secretary)
David Coates
Allan Cochrane
Jeremy Cooper (BBC)
Neil Costello
Clare Falkner (BBC)
Stuart Hall
Susan Himmelweit
Jack Leathem (BBC)
Richard Maidment
Doreen Massey
Gregor McLennan
Andrew Northedge
Kay Pole
Marilyn Ricci (Course Manager)
Paul Smith
Richard Stevens
Elaine Storkey
Kenneth Thompson
Diane Watson
Margaret Wetherell

External Consultants
Tom Burden
David Deacon
David Denver
Caroline Dumonteil
Owen Hartley
Tom Hulley
Robert Looker
Angela Phillips
Colm Regan
Richard Sanders
Neil Thompson
Patrick Wright

Tutor Assessors
Alan Brown
Lyn Brennan
Mona Clark
Ian Crosher
Donna Dickenson
Brian Graham
Philip Markey
Norma Sherratt
Jan Vance

Tom Hunter, Chris Wooldridge, David Wilson, Robert Cookson, Nigel Draper, David Scott-Macnab (Editors); Paul Smith (Librarian); Alison George (Graphic Artist); Jane Sheppard (Designer); Sue Rippon and Mollie Hancock (Project Control); Robin Thornton (Summer School Manager); John Hunt (IT for Summer School); John Bennett and others.

External Academic Assessors
Professor Anthony Giddens, Cambridge University (Overall Course Assessor)
Dr Geoffrey Harcourt, Cambridge University (Block III)
Dr Patrick Dunleavy, London School of Economics and Political Science (Block IV)
Dr Halla Beloff, Edinburgh University (Block V)
Professor Brian Robson, Manchester University (Block VI)

The Open University,

Walton Hall,

Milton Keynes, MK7 6AA

First published 1991; Second Edition 1995. Reprinted 1995

© 1995 The Open University

Edited, designed and typeset by The Open University.

Printed in the United Kingdom by Alden, Oxford, Didcot and Northampton.

ISBN 0 7492 0182 7

This text forms part of an Open University Foundation Level Course D103 *Society and Social Science: a Foundation Course*. If you would like a copy of *Studying with the Open University*, please write to the Central Enquiry Service, PO Box 200, The Open University, Walton Hall, Milton Keynes, MK7 6YZ, United Kingdom.

BLOCK INTRODUCTION AND STUDY GUIDE

Prepared for the Course Team by Vivienne Brown

Welcome to Block III 'Work, markets and the economy'. In this block we are going to look at the economy and some major economic issues of the 1990s. You have already looked at some aspects of the economy in earlier parts of the course but in this block we are going to concentrate on the economy as a whole.

An important issue threading its way through this block concerns the factors determining the growth of an economy. What enables an economy to grow fast and provide increases in living standards? Unit 10 addresses this question by looking at work. It asks the question 'What is work?' and finds that there are many different kinds of work which are essential to the functioning of an economy. There is the paid work that goes on in factories, offices and shops. There is also the unpaid work that goes on inside households, caring for children, washing clothes, cooking meals and so on. There are also unpaid voluntary workers such as school governors, justices of the peace, charity workers and so on. Most economic analyses take into account only the first kind of work, paid work in the public domain, but even here some kinds of work have been regarded as more productive than others in contributing to economic growth. Unit 10 critically reviews these debates and considers why some sectors in the economy have been regarded as more important sources of growth than others. While studying this unit you will be able to watch TV 05 which looks at women and work.

One of the distinctions made in Unit 10 concerns those activities that are performed within a market context and those that are not. Unit 11 picks up on this by looking at competitive markets. One of the arguments in favour of markets is that competitive markets impose a strict financial discipline on firms, forcing them to be efficient, and that this tends to promote economic growth. Criticisms of markets challenge this by arguing that there are many hidden — and not so hidden — costs involved in market activities and that these seriously detract from market efficiency. One such cost is the unemployment that seems endemic to market economies. Another cost takes the form of side effects of market activities (known as 'externalities') whose implications cannot be captured within the price system. An important example of this is pollution. Another criticism of markets is that they lead to gross inequalities in the distribution of life chances. These inequalities are inefficient in that they prevent people from realizing their full potential, but it is argued that they are also unfair and militate against basic ideas of social justice.

Unit 12 examines the role for government policy in managing the aggregate economy or macroeconomy as an overall economic system. An important objective of government policy is a high and stable level of economic growth along with low inflation and low unemployment, but the actual performance of any economy often falls far below its potential. Further, the emphasis in the past decade or so has shifted towards emphasizing the overriding importance of aiming for low inflation at the possible cost of rising unemployment and falling growth. This unit analyses the debate between monetarists and Keynesians over the scope for demand management policies. It also considers the increased attention that is now being devoted to what are called 'supply side' issues which are concerned with the productive potential of the economy. Finally, the unit examines a marxist discussion about the longer term influences on the performance of the UK economy. The television programme scheduled alongside this unit (TV 06) looks at instances of privatization in the UK during the 1980s.

Another important issue for this block concerns the ways in which the traditions of social thought have shaped our understandings of the economy. This issue is considered in Units 11 and 12. Unit 11 examines liberal arguments in favour of markets and then goes on to examine some social reformist critiques of the liberal position. Two Reader chapters have been selected to provide examples of liberal and social reformist writings on the virtues and shortcomings of free markets. You will also be asked to read a section from Chapter 22 of the Course Reader on the liberal approach to economy and society. Whereas Unit 11 looks at different traditions of thought mainly from the standpoint of 'microeconomics' or individual markets, Unit 12 considers them from the point of view of 'macroeconomics' which concerns the functioning of the overall economy. This unit also examines the influence of the traditions on economic analysis by looking at the ways in which different approaches to government macroeconomic policy reflect different traditions of thought. During your reading of Unit 12 you will be asked to read further sections from Chapter 22 on social reformism and marxism.

The course themes also feature in this block. The most important theme here is the theme of 'representation and reality'. In each of the units you will find that different economic models are being used: in Unit 10 different models of productive labour are examined; in Unit 11 different models of competitive markets are analysed; and in Unit 12 different models of the macroeconomy are explored. As you will see, all of these models have direct policy implications. In addition to providing a review of Block III, Unit 13 then provides a moment to pause and consider some of the ways in which economic models are constructed and used. This unit also builds on Unit 9 and the discussion there of the role of concepts in social science thinking.

Another course theme which surfaces in this block is that of the different distinctions between the 'public and the private'. Unit 10 discusses this in relation to the different fields of work, and the theme also features prominently in Unit 12's discussion of government economic policy. Finally, the 'local and the global' is touched on in Unit 10 and is then treated more fully in Unit 12's discussion of the international position of the UK economy.

Whilst reading Unit 10, you will be asked to read Chapter 7 of the Reader 'The future of work' by Alan Warde which looks at the impact of new technologies and increased competition on the ways in which work is organized. For Unit 11 there are the two Reader articles representing a liberal and a social reformist approach to markets. The first, 'Competitive markets and economic freedom' by Milton Friedman (Chapter 8) presents a liberal defence of markets. The second, 'The economic question and the larger social scene' by John Kenneth Galbraith (Chapter 9) provides a social reformist critique of markets and of mass unemployment. Finally, there are two chapters associated with Unit 12. 'British growth over the long run' by Nick Crafts (Chapter 10) sets out some broad questions about UK growth, and also contains statistics and arguments that are relevant to Unit 10. The final chapter is 'Theories of decline' by Bernard Stafford (Chapter 11) which reviews a marxist debate about the sources of long run decline in the UK economy.

As with other blocks in D103, this block also includes two radio programmes. Radio 05 will investigate various aspects of different economies. Radio 06 is scheduled alongside Unit 13 and will offer advice on TMA 03. There is also an audio-cassette to help you study the diagrams in Units 11 and 12 at your own pace.

The principal study skill that you will be working on for this block is that of essay writing and it builds on Chapter 6, Section 4 of *The Good Study Guide*. The Study Skills Section has been scheduled to come in Week 11 and you will find it at the end of Unit 11.

UPDATING THE COURSE

There is plenty of scope for you to update the course as you are studying it. One possibility is for you to identify one or two major issues in Block III that you are particularly interested in, and then to use your *resource file* to keep newspaper articles on these issues. Some potential candidates that come to mind here are: changes in the rate of growth; changes in employment; changes in inequality; results of forming the single European market; government economic policy, for example privatization, interest rate policy, exchange rate policy, the budget and inflation.

It is also worth checking to see if there are *Endnotes* to this block with updating material.

STUDY TIME ALLOCATIONS

In the Study Guide below, we have listed all the components of Block III with time allocations to help you plan your study time over the four weeks.

Block components	Approximate study time (hours)
Block introduction and Study Guide	$\frac{1}{2}$
Unit 10: Work and the economy	$6\frac{1}{2}$
TV 05: Women, Children and work	2
Reader: Chapter 7	2
Total	11
Unit 11: Competitive markets	6
Reader: Chapters 8 and 9	$2\frac{1}{2}$
Reader: Chapter 22, Section 2.1 'Liberalism'	1
Radio 05	$\frac{1}{2}$
Audio-cassette 3	$\frac{1}{2}$
Study Skills Section: Good writing 1	2
The Good Study Guide: Chapter 6, Section 4	
Total	$12\frac{1}{2}$
Unit 12: The management of the UK economy	6
TV 06: From public to private	2
Reader: Chapters 10 and 11	3
Reader: Chapter 22, parts of Sections 2.2 and 2.3 'Social Reformism' and 'Marxism'.	1
Audio-cassette 3	$\frac{1}{2}$
Total	$12\frac{1}{2}$
Unit 13: Constructing models	$3\frac{1}{2}$
Radio 06	$\frac{1}{2}$
TMA 03	6
Total	10

UNIT 10   WORK AND THE ECONOMY

Prepared for the Course Team by Susan Himmelweit and Neil Costello

CONTENTS

1   INTRODUCTION

This unit is mainly about work. As the first unit of Block III it has, however, also a wider agenda of exploring the economy and economic processes through the prism of work. Looking at work will enable us to:

1   start examining some specific features of the modern economy such as its division of labour;

2   see what work is necessary to keep the economy going and the contribution different types of work make to the economy; and

3   examine some of the ways in which a capitalist economy organizes and allocates work.

Further, we also aim to give you an initial feel for the discipline of economics by:

4   introducing some of the terms economists use and the distinctions they make; and

5   examining some economic theories and using different styles of economic argument.

We shall do all this in a number of different ways. The unit has three main sections, each including a number of activities — it is important you do these if you are to get the most out of this unit. The sections of the unit differ not only in their subject matter, but also in their mode of argument, shifting gear and style of exposition between sections.

The first section is a rather discursive one, exploring the meaning of the term 'work' in the modern economy. This may seem a fairly straightforward task, but it will prove more complex than it seems and will lead us to examine a number of different economic aspects of society: its division of labour, the process of exchange and the distinctions between paid and unpaid labour, and between public and private.

The next section uses a different method of exploration. It is more empirical, looking at three specific types of work which are typical of the British economy as it appears at the end of the twentieth century. One of the examples is actually no work — unemployment — whereas the others are jobs which have changed a great deal over the last two or three decades. However, this section is not merely descriptive. To make sense of the world around us a choice has to be made as to which empirical facts are presented. So the examples of work selected have been chosen to enable us to explore more general questions about work: what it means to us as individuals, how it is organized, and how it is gendered in Britain today.

At the end of Section 2, we ask you to adopt another mode of study, using a published article. 'The future of work' by Alan Warde, Chapter 7 of the Reader, summarizes and assesses arguments claiming that there has recently been a substantial shift in the nature of work in the economy. We shall then be asking you, in turn, to assess Warde's argument.

Section 3 shifts gear again. It is explicitly theoretical, looking at and comparing different economic theories of which work creates wealth. But theories cannot be judged on theoretical grounds alone, so there are some empirical questions posed in this section and we shall also be looking at the policy implications of the different theories. At the end of this section we return to the division between public and private domains to see how an economist's definition of work may have hidden implications even for those whose work is unrecognized by economic theory.

By the end of the unit we hope you will not only have learnt a bit about work and its different meanings, but also have begun your study of the economy and the work of economists which the other units in this block will continue.

1.1 WHAT IS WORK?

Let us start by thinking about the meaning of work, what it represents to us. It is clearly something very important in our society, so important that we use it to define ourselves and other people. If asked 'What do you do?', you are much more likely to reply that you are a plumber, a secretary or a managing director than to talk about any of the myriad other activities which you spend time doing but which are not seen as work. Our work in that sense defines us all.

Similarly, as we shall discover, the way work is organized to a large extent defines our economy and the meaning of economic activity. To explore this let us first look at what is meant by 'work'.

ACTIVITY 1

Here is a list of different ways in which people spend time. For each activity think about whether you would classify it as work. And think about your reasons for saying that it is or is not to count as 'work':

- giving birth
- looking after children
- teaching
- studying with the Open University
- writing an Open University Unit
- writing a play
- writing lists and filling in forms
- working on the assembly line at a factory
- running a factory
- running a trade union
- running a tennis club
- running a shop
- shopping
- cooking
- eating
- playing football
- growing flowers
- making a path
- making a road
- driving along a road
- catching speeding motorists as a policeman
- sitting on a bench as a magistrate

Is this work?

You probably found it quite difficult to decide which activities to call work. You may have felt that there was not enough information about some of the items on the list to classify them. One could say, for example, that it depends who the children are as to whether looking after them is to count as work or not. When you look after your own children that is not seen as work, but if you employ a child minder to look after them that is her job and for her it is work. Other activities from the list might sometimes be seen as work and at other times as enjoyable pastimes. For example, a market gardener who grows flowers to sell is more likely to see it as work than an amateur pursuing gardening as a hobby for its own sake. Similarly, some onerous tasks may count as work in some contexts but not in others. Writing lists and filling in forms is part of a clerical worker's job but it is also a chore most of us have to do at various times without considering it to be our work.

If you made those sort of distinctions then you have noticed something very important about activities: that it is not what you are doing but the *social context* in which it is done which determines whether we see a particular activity as work or not. The meaning of an activity, whether it counts as work, depends largely on the relation between the person doing it and the people or organization for whom it is done. For example, the relation between a woman and her children is a different type of social relation from that she has with her employer. This will affect the meaning she puts on the activities she performs in the context of her family or her employment. The *social context* includes the social relations under which an activity is performed, but also has a wider connotation and refers to the whole social framework in which an activity is done, in particular, the reason why it is being done: for enjoyment, to please a friend, to avoid getting into trouble or to earn a wage, to name but a few reasons why we do things.

So, by this criterion, it is not the actual content of activities, what physical movements are needed, how much thought goes into them or how much energy is expended, that determines whether or not they count as work. Rather we classify activities according to the social context in which they take place and in particular the reason why they are being done. Driving a car, for example, is work if it is part of your job, but driving the same car along the same route at the same time will not be counted as work if you are taking the family out for the day.

—————————————————— ACTIVITY 2 ——————————————————

The notion of one person doing exactly the same activity, such as planting the same flowers or driving a car at the same time along the same route both as work and non-work (or leisure) is actually a bit far fetched. We are unlikely to do this. Can you think why that is?

Work and non-work activities are distinguished in a number of different ways. First we tend to have particular times at which we work. Even the self-employed, who could work at any time, often set aside particular periods as work time and leisure time. Similarly the places at which we work tend to be distinct from those at which we do not; most people think of themselves as going out to work and spending much of their leisure time at home. And we tend to reinforce those distinctions even when they are not necessary. So we may, for example, like to avoid making the journey that we make to work at other times. The distinction between work and non-work has an important cultural meaning in our society.

But are you perhaps feeling a bit uneasy by now? Are you sure you agree with the definition of work implicitly being used? We seem to be assuming that work must be done to bring in money; we keep talking about work as though it has to be part of a job — except in the case of the market gardener, but in that case the aim was to make money too. And we used as our examples of non-work similar activities that did not bring in money. But not everyone would draw the distinction in the same way.

The way we have implicitly defined it above to mean an activity done to bring in money does reflect one way in which the term 'work' is used in everyday speech. When asked, 'Do you work?', people who are extremely busy but are not paid may reply, 'No, I've got three small children, I haven't got any time to work' or 'No, I retired last year and can now spend my time doing the things I've always wanted to'. Answers like these imply that work has to be something whose main purpose is to bring in money, unlike things that you do simply because they need doing or for enjoyment. By this definition none of the following would count as work: all forms of housework in one's own home, looking after one's own children or elderly relatives, helping a neighbour out with any of these for no pay, cleaning one's own windows or voluntary community work such as running a tennis club. But, on the other hand, the same activities, doing housework for someone else and being paid for it, being employed in a private nursery or by the local council in an old people's home, window-cleaning as one's own business, or running a tennis club as a paid manager would all count as work because they bring in money.

But this is not the only way 'work' could be defined. The same people who denied that they worked above, if asked how they spend their time, may well reply: 'Bringing up three small children is very hard work, I'm on the go all day and have to fit the housework in when I can' or 'I do a lot of voluntary work and there are always bits of work to do in the garden'. In these cases the term 'work' is being used more in the sense of useful or necessary activity rather than reflecting whether it brings in money or not. Not all 'work' defined in this sense brings in money, despite the fact that some of these types of work are just as necessary to society as those that do.

—————————————— ACTIVITY 3 ——————————————

Make a list of work that is done which does not bring in money, but is necessary for the running of society.

Many important institutions in society depend on voluntary labour: school governors, justices of the peace, hospital visitors, charity workers, local community activists, members of pressure groups and political parties all put in a great deal of unpaid time. The education system, the judiciary, the health service, charitable institutions, community and national politics are all essential to the way our society runs. And all these social institutions depend on volunteers, whose work, because unpaid, would not be counted as economic activity by official statistics. Whether the time spent counts as 'work' depends on which view of work one takes, but there can be little doubt that society could not function in the way it does without such voluntary labour. And further, given the way our health care, education, judicial and political systems are run, the labour of those volunteers is a necessary complement to the work of those who do paid labour for the same institutions.

Important though the 'voluntary sector' is, a much more significant site of unpaid labour is the home. Nearly everybody does some form of housework, though there is a huge variation in the amount done by different people. Much of the work that is done within households is concerned with the daily living of people, shopping, cooking their meals, providing them with clean clothes and somewhere warm and comfortable to relax and sleep. Such activities and their results enable people to go on living and, in particular, to work. It is part of their individual regeneration or *reproduction*.

Other work that is done at home revolves around the creation of a new generation. Childbirth and subsequent child care is also necessary for the reproduction of people, in a more long term sense. Most people who perform all the different types of domestic work that contribute to the *reproduction of people* are unpaid, but their labour is essential for society to continue. Without people after all there would be no society. Such 'work' may go almost unrecognized, but it is nevertheless vital to the continuation of society.

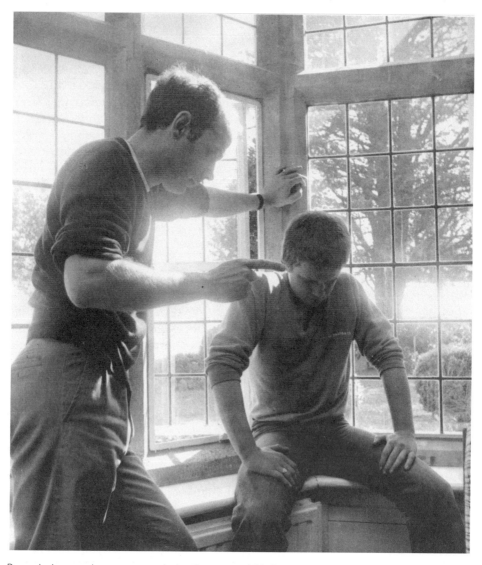

Reproducing people means reproducing them as social beings

'Reproduction', however, can mean more than just the reproduction of people. We can also talk about the *reproduction of society*, by which we mean those processes which are necessary for society to carry on. This includes the reproduction of the next generation, but it has a much broader meaning encompassing all that is necessary to enable society to continue in its present form. As well as domestic labour, all those forms of necessary voluntary labour that we mentioned above are therefore part of the process of reproducing society. So, indeed, is much paid labour: not only the labour that produces food and other necessities of life, but all the labour that produces the goods and services that make our society the way it is. Our society would be very different if there was no work done to write books, send out bills, print voting papers and educate our children, to name but a few examples.

So now we have two meanings of the term 'work': one of them refers just to work done for money whereas the other usage of the term encompasses all activities necessary for the reproduction of society whether paid or not. Both correspond to ways in which the term 'work' can be used in everyday speech.

By the first definition, the content of the activity is irrelevant; it is the social context in which it is done that defines it as 'work'. This is underlined by the tendency in our society for clear distinctions of time, place and attitude to be drawn between 'work' and 'non-work' in this first sense.

In the second sense, 'work' includes a number of activities that bring in no money to the person doing it, but are nevertheless important or necessary to society. Here it is the content of the work done that is significant and it may be done in different social contexts, for example be paid or unpaid, and still count as work.

ACTIVITY 4

We have looked at a number of examples that do not count as work in our first sense because they are not done for money, but do count in the second sense of being important to society. What about the other way round? Can you think of activities for which people are paid which are not necessary to the reproduction of society?

We can all probably think of some examples, but we may well not agree on what these are. Working on the production of weapons, in advertising or the tobacco industry are examples that some people might cite of work that, while it may be well paid, does no good or even positive harm to society. Other people may disagree with these particular examples but nearly everyone would agree that not all paid work is necessarily beneficial to society. But whether an activity is beneficial is a different issue from whether it is necessary to the reproduction of the sort of society in which we live today. Some economists argue that state expenditure on arms is necessary to keep a capitalist economy going. Indeed economists, interested in the question of how wealth is created, have, for more than two centuries, argued over which jobs contribute to the wealth upon which our economy's growth and prosperity depends. This is an important theoretical question which has great significance for the formulation of economic policy and one to which we shall return in Section 3 of this unit.

SUMMARY

There are two meanings of the term 'work' used in everyday speech:

* work which is done in order to bring in money as payment to the person doing it;

or

* any activity that contributes to the reproduction of society, that is, is necessary for society to run in the way it does.

These two definitions do not amount to the same thing. A great deal of work that is useful to society is not paid for, in particular domestic labour which contributes to the reproduction of people, and thus to society, is usually unpaid.

1.2   EXCHANGE AND THE DIVISION OF LABOUR

Is it rather curious that we have these two meanings of the term 'work'? Let us explore a bit further why we need them both.

The second notion of work as an activity that does something useful for society is a definition that could be applied to any society. Of course, what is considered useful in different societies can vary quite a bit; different types of societies need different work to be done to keep them going. Huge armies of labour have always been needed to build irrigation works in many Asian countries, but their work would not be considered useful in a climate where it rains all the year round. Teaching children to add pounds, shillings and pence used to be part of the work involved in the reproduction of British society; children had to grow up able to operate the monetary system of their own country. But that work is no longer necessary, nor would it ever have been in countries with a decimal system of currency. Which activities are necessary for the reproduction of society will vary across societies and historically within societies. Nevertheless, despite such variation in what is considered useful, the notion of judging whether an activity should count as 'work' by whether it contributes to society is one that can be applied in any society.

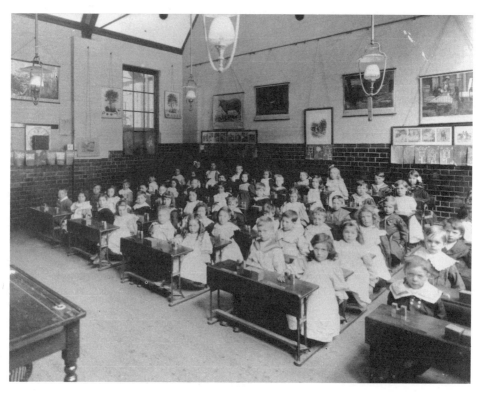

'Teaching children to add pounds, shillings and pence used to be part of the work involved in the reproduction of British society'

This is quite unlike our first definition of 'work' as paid activity. This definition can only be applied in some sorts of societies, those that have a system of *exchange*, involving money and paid labour. In Britain, as in all capitalist economies, we have a highly developed system of exchange. In fact much of society runs by it, so it is worth examining the exchange process in more detail.

An exchange is an agreement between two parties, entered into because each wants to get something from the other. In a capitalist economy, workers need money on which to live and employers need workers to work in their enterprises; they therefore enter into an exchange and workers sell their ability to labour for a wage. Similarly, self-employed people receive the money they need to live by selling the products of their labour for money. Shopping is another example of the exchange process; when you shop you pay money in order to buy goods and services and the shopkeeper sells you what you want in order to get money. When money is involved, an exchange is a sale from the point of view of one party and a purchase from the point of view of the other.

Exchange is an important economic activity because in modern Britain much of the division of labour is carried out by exchange. A society's *division of labour* refers to the way in which people in that society can specialize in doing particular types of work but consume the products of other people's labour. Exchange is one way that a division of labour can be carried out between people who have no other connection with each other. In Unit 1, you saw how international exchange, or trade as it was called there, allowed for a global division of labour whereby goods produced in one place could be consumed on the other side of the world. Similarly, exchange can carry out a division of labour within a society.

It is through the *market*, a general term for the buying and selling of goods and services, that the products of different people's labour can be exchanged. A well-developed system of exchange allows people to earn an income by specializing in one sort of production or another, safe in the knowledge that all the other goods and services that they need, but do not produce themselves, will be available on the market. In other words, the development of the market enables a division of labour between specialist producers to occur.

Exchange is not the only way a division of labour is carried out in our economy. Within most workplaces, not all workers do the same job or produce the whole product. There is therefore an internal division of labour too. In a capitalist enterprise, the internal division of labour is organized by the management who employ workers to do particular jobs as part of the overall production process. The division of labour carried on by the market is rather different: no-one organizes it overall, people just engage in the particular purchases and sales in which they are interested. Nevertheless, the outcome is a vast and complex division of labour throughout the whole of society, which is often talked about as the social division of labour to distinguish it from the internal division of labour that goes on within workplaces.

These two different types of division of labour in our capitalist economy are rather like its two different notions of work. In all societies there is some division of labour, but not all societies have a social division of labour carried on by exchange. In some the division of labour may be regulated more by custom and rights, as under feudalism, for example, where a serf had an obligation to work for his lord and also, in some cases, for the church. The process of exchange, and in particular that of exchange for money, is a social process, a feature of particular types of society. Other societies may organize their division of labour differently; if they do they will be very different sorts of societies and have very different notions of work.

But the development of the international market has meant that in most of the world today some, at least, of the division of labour is regulated by exchange and some, at least, of the work carried out in society is done for money. As Unit 1 pointed out, trade has been a very powerful social force, swamping other ways of regulating the division of labour so that the production of commodities for the market and, in particular, capitalist commodity production has tended to eclipse other forms of work. This is true not only on a world-wide scale, but, as we shall see in the next section, also has important effects on the way work is perceived and organized within our own economy.

> ### SUMMARY
> - Exchange allows a social division of labour among specialist producers to take place through the market.
> - Exchange is not the only way a division of labour can be carried out. Other types of societies have different ways of organizing their social division of labour. And within our society, most workplaces have an organized internal division of labour too, but exchange is the main way in which the labour of society as a whole is divided.

1.3   PUBLIC AND PRIVATE DOMAINS

There is, as we have already mentioned, a great deal of work, according to our second definition of the term, that goes on in households. It is mostly service work: caring for children, washing clothes, cooking meals, making beds and so on. Though similar services can be purchased, when performed for the family in the home such work does not reach the market.

ACTIVITY 5

If asked the question with which we began this unit, 'What do you do?', why do you think some women with small children to look after and a house to run reply that they are 'only' housewives?

I think that 'only' comes from the existence of those two definitions of 'work'. As we noted earlier, our work is how we define ourselves if we have a paid job. A housewife certainly works in the second sense of contributing to the reproduction of society, but she does not have a job. Her belittling of her status as 'only' a housewife reflects in this way the ambivalence of society to her work, needing it but failing to give it any public recognition. Let us explore a bit further why this happens.

A housewife is not paid for the work she does. This means that her work gives her no direct access to money nor therefore to the products of society that one needs money to buy, for which she is dependent on other members of her household. Further, because money is the way our society values activities, work which is unpaid receives less recognition than paid work, so much so that according to one of our definitions it does not even count as 'work'.

In practice, there are not that many full-time housewives in Britain today. As we shall see later in this unit, most women are in employment most of their adult lives, although many interrupt or change their employment patterns while they have children at home. But whether or not women also have jobs, they tend to do the majority of work within the household including most of the child care. And whoever it is done by, housework does not receive the same recognition as paid work in our society.

Not only is housework unpaid, but also its products are not put up for sale. Instead, people perform housework for the direct consumption and benefit of themselves and their families. This means that their work does not become part of the *social* division of labour, the division of labour which takes place through the exchange of products through the market. The division of labour in housework is a small-scale *private* one between members of the household, allocated usually according to a customary gender division.

As you will have seen already in this course from Unit 1 onwards, there are many ways in which our society can be divided into *public* and *private* domains. As far as work is concerned, exchange marks a crucial boundary between public and private. The labour process within firms is organized internally but as soon as its products are sold the labour that went into them becomes part of society's overall division of labour. So work that produces commodities receives public recognition when those commodities are sold. On the other hand, reproductive work within the household remains within the private domain, does not receive that public recognition and does not get a valuation by society's measure of money; it is not paid nor is its output sold.

A great deal of time and effort, however, goes into reproductive work and our society would be a very different one if all that work was recognized and had to be paid for. As I write now in 1990, employers facing a shortage of certain types of skilled labour have been considering various schemes to encourage more women with small children to stay in or return to employment. To do so they have to find some way of substituting for the large amount of work that they would otherwise be doing unpaid in the home. TV05 will consider the difficulties and costs of substituting for unpaid reproductive work in a particularly crucial area — the care of pre-school children.

SUMMARY

- For work, exchange marks the boundary between public and private domains.
- Work in the private domain does not enter into the social division of labour because its products are not exchanged but consumed directly.
- Reproductive work in the private domain does not receive the public recognition of money despite its importance to society. The financial contribution of wage-earners tends to be more recognized than the housework they or other members of the household do, even though both are equally important to the way the household runs and the life-styles of its members and, indeed, to the reproduction of society as a whole.

---

2   THE WORLD OF WORK

This section of the unit is about the experience of work. We are going to move away from the more abstract concerns of the last section to a number of largely descriptive accounts of aspects of work. There are theoretical issues behind these accounts, as you will see, but as you read this section you should reflect upon your own experience and think about questions such as the ones below.

Do you find yourself under similar pressures to those described? How much autonomy do you have and why? How structured is your work? Do you have to do largely those things other people tell you to do? How much status do you have? Are there distinct differences in the work carried out by men and women? If so, what sort of differences are these and why do you think they arise? Whom do you work with — men or women or both? Are your workmates from different ethnic backgrounds? Do you work only for money or are there other reasons for working?

If questions occur to you as you read, note them down and perhaps discuss them at your next tutorial.

2.1   UNEMPLOYMENT

A full-time housewife has no income of her own and this has a number of implications, as we saw at the end of the last section. Unemployed men find themselves in much the same position. They also lack the status of working in the public domain and frequently find themselves on the edge of society, unable to participate fully. If we consider the experiences of someone who is unemployed we can gain insight into the meaning of work and the way work, or the lack of it, structures our interaction with the rest of the world.

The article below, which is reproduced from *The Guardian,* was written by a man who had experienced long periods of unemployment over a period of about ten years. His article is not a balanced, disinterested account of the impact of unemployment on some other person, nor is it meant to be. It is a partisan, deeply-felt plea for greater understanding of the plight of unemployed people. It challenges conventional views about the experience and causes of unemployment and it makes a number of bold political statements. It does not claim to set out all there is to say about unemployment and it is not in any sense a survey of all the ways in which unemployment can affect people's lives. It is a powerful piece of writing, however, and worthy of consideration as an account of what unemployment feels like and, implicitly, how it relates to an individual's connection with the wider society.

———————————————— ACTIVITY 6 ————————————————

In a moment you should read Jim Jarratt's article on unemployment. As you do so keep these two questions in mind:

1   What are the main things which Jim Jarratt appears to lack as a result of his employment history?
2   What are the different ways unemployment and its effects are represented?

Now turn to Jim Jarratt's article.

The lack of money lies at the heart of Jim Jarratt's 'cry from the wilderness'. He and his family have a restricted diet because of this. They argue more and find their social lives impoverished. They cannot take part in activities which are taken for granted by those more fortunate and, with cruel irony, even if part-time work is available the social benefit rules are such that he cannot consider supplementing his income, he can only replace it. This is sometimes referred to as the *poverty trap*. The need for money is absolutely central to the circumstances in which Jim Jarratt finds himself and, not surprisingly, the lack of money comes across as the major impact of unemployment.

It is not only the lack of money which creates problems for the unemployed, however. Jim Jarratt describes himself as 'one of the untouchables of the British caste system'. He talks about the views of some employers that unemployed equals unemployable. He feels insulted and embarrassed by requests on job application forms for details of his current job. The lack of paid employment, for him, makes a statement about the way in which society perceives his worth. Without paid work he senses that society sees him as undesirable. 'Lives are blasted', he says, 'and talent is flushed down the drain'. His own sense of personal worth is continually undermined and this is exacerbated by the real lack of understanding of what it feels like to be caught in this trap. 'The politician who signed on the dole for a month and said it "wasn't bad" is beneath contempt...such people have no knowledge of what it means to be a second class citizen...'. So we can see that the experience of unemployment is much more than being without money. The lack of any financial security is absolutely central to the difficulties created by unemployment but its effects go deep into the ways in which individuals perceive themselves, and into the ways in which they are themselves perceived by the wider society.

Government surplus

You've never had it so good . . . The old maestro's slogan has been paraphrased by our present Prime Minister. But she'd better not try saying it to **Jim Jarratt**

THE THATCHER miracle has worked. Unemployment is falling, people are getting back to work, and everything is rosy in the garden. But I don't believe it.

The paltry fall in local unemployment statistics is constantly outstripped by redundancies as more and more local businesses close down. Good, once secure, jobs are lost while the few new jobs generated in the area often dwell in the realms of long hours and low pay. I recently encountered a vacancy for a packer offering £1 an hour for a 40-hour week. Such wages would be unacceptable in the affluent South-East, but in the North the values of the workhouse and the mill master are starting to prevail.

Things are getting better, I am told. I don't believe it. I have been struggling to find a job since being made redundant six months ago and it's damn near impossible. Not that unemployment is new to me. I secured my last job as a supervisor on Pennine Heritage's Countryside Taskforce in the autumn of 1987; previously I had been struggling to find a job for four years. At Pennine Heritage I had the chance to recover my self respect, get back to a normal lifestyle, and take the family on holiday, before I lost my job as a result of MSC funding being phased out to make way for Employment Training.

Everybody thinks ET is a good idea except those who have the misfortune to be coerced on to it. The unemployed are not consulted about what they want. They are presented with a fait accompli designed to be more of benefit to employers than the unemployed.

As the rest of society goes its merry way, the unemployed, like their paymasters, are forced to dwell in a world of "stealth and total obscurity" Surplus to requirements, the poor, the defenceless, the inarticulate, and, in the eyes of some, "the shiftless and bone idle" are the untouchables of the British caste system.

I am one of those untouchables, part of that Government surplus which has no place in the structure of things, cut off from the rest of society because I have no adequate answer to the eternal opening gambit of "what do you do for a living?" I am tarred with the brush and bound by the fetters of "can't get a job".

Why not? I have asked that question many times and have never been able to come up with a simple answer. I am articulate, well educated (a one-time student teacher). In my youth I worked as an actor/musician, appeared on radio and TV, and published a book of my songs. In the 80s I left all that to settle down and start a family, just in time to discover that jobs were no longer easy to come by. Moving from scheme to government scheme, I have been going around the system since 1979.

In 1983, after being made redundant from a supervisory post which I lost as a result of YOPS being phased out for YTS (you see I've been here before), I began writing, to try to hang on to my self respect and give my life some sense of purpose. After an endless succession of rejection letters from would-be employers and publishers alike, after raised hopes and bitter disappointments, I managed to secure both a publisher for one of my manuscripts and the job at Pennine Heritage. I might be forgiven for thinking that my boat had come in and at last my family would be able to live a normal life.

Not so. On the dole once more, I can give my time to entertaining schoolkids or giving the odd lecture about my book, yet I cannot get a job sweeping the streets.

It's not for want of trying. With a wife and three young children at home, getting a job becomes an obsession. Failure is not disappointment, it is heartbreak. Week by week the dole gets harder to live on and the family diet becomes increasingly basic, being an endless round of toast, jam, baked beans, sausages and chips, all those "unhealthy foods" Edwina Currie says we shouldn't eat. It must be nice to have a choice.

Income Support is barely enough to live on. Neither my wife nor I smoke or drink, and I shudder to think of the lifestyle of those who do. Our clothes come from jumble sales or from the generosity of grandparents who have to live on a pittance themselves, but are willing to put their grandchildren before their own comforts.

Everything runs down on the dole. If the washer breaks down or the vacuum packs up, it's either fix it yourself or dump it — there is no way you can afford a replacement, unless you wish to lower yourself to the level of taking a Social Fund loan, and all the aggravation which that entails. Things like home improvements are but a pipe dream. You have enough, with very careful management, to keep on top of the bills and to buy essentials, and that's it. There is no progression through life, no future, just stagnation and slow decay.

Arguments increase within the household, along with bitterness, anger and recriminations. Relationships break down, marriages go on the rocks. Suicide is considered, and, in some cases, carried out. There is no money to plan holidays, to take the kids for a day at the seaside. School trips and outings become a financial embarrassment, and the children cannot understand why they cannot go with their classmates. Unemployment reaps a harvest of social division and domestic discord. You lose touch with friends and they with you. You cannot live up to their lifestyles and they cannot see why.

The gulf between the employed and the jobless is a vast one; not only financially but in terms of understanding. Those who have never known long-term unemployment can have no idea what it is like. The politician who signed on the dole for a month and said it "wasn't bad" is beneath contempt. It would take two years for a man of his means to even notice his lifestyle was slipping. Such people have no knowledge of what it means to be a second-class citizen who cannot get credit or legally supplement his income by working part time. (Anything in excess of £4 a week comes off benefit.) This hardly encourages the unemployed to seek part-time work, and job sharing is a joke to the very people it is supposed to help. There is no way, short of finding a full-time, well-paid job that the unemployed can be significantly better off.

Much of Employment Training is but free labour for employers masquerading as trainers, filling the gap left by the inadequacies of public sector education establishments, which are only inadequate because they have been deliberately underfunded in the first place. Starving, they have gone with the begging bowl to the mighty MSC, and now, completely under the control of government bureaucracy, Maggie has pulled the plug on them so the profiteers can move in. That education for all, which our forefathers struggled so hard to attain, is now cast upon the winds of exploitation and greed.

Employment Training is really about the convenient laundering of unemployment statistics and exploitation of unemployed labour for benefit plus £10. People are coerced on to it with threats of loss of benefit. It is the thin end of a wedge which will lead to the shadow of the workhouse and the labour camp. The unemployed live in a prison without bars.

So go out! Get a job — or some training! I've already done so. I have secured certificates in business computing, drystone walling, and first aid. None of these monkey metal qualifications has helped me get a job. Because getting a job is a job in itself, I have a phone, a typewriter, an immaculate computer-generated CV (continually updated), and a regular supply of newspapers from every town in the region. In six months I have applied for nearly 40 jobs. I have had four interviews. I am still unemployed.

On 90 per cent of application forms, I am insulted and embarrassed by being asked for details of my present job, the implication being that if you are not leaving a job to go to theirs, you are not worthy of consideration. This prejudice of employers in favour of the already employed explains why when jobs are advertised in hundreds, unemployment statistics only fall in tens. The unemployed aren't getting the jobs, only schemes. The employed are going round and round in circles chasing after each other's jobs. The unemployed can't get a look in because, in the eyes of employers, unemployed equals unemployable.

Employers have it all their own way. They can draw the best staff from their competitors and man the bottom line with conscript labour from the dole queues. No one objects in communities which are desperate for job creation at any price

Being a teacher or a doctor is a career. Being an assembly-line operative is a job you do for the acquisition of money. It's amazing how many employers and people in authority do not seem to know the difference. Recently I was refused a job as a proof-reader on a newspaper on the grounds that someone of my experience and background would find this work boring and unfulfilling. I was annoyed, as this would-be-employer obviously had no understanding of the priorities of people on the dole, who I am sure would be more than willing to be unfulfilled for £170 a week. What the unemployed need is not a job at any price, but any job at a good price.

I am nearly 40 which, as far as the jobs market is concerned, makes me a job-seeking geriatric. Jobs and courses I apply for frequently have an upper age limit of 30. This is commonplace in a market where employers seek "qualified and experienced staff" under the age of 25. If I were black, or a woman, I could cry discrimination. Not that that makes much difference either.

Qualifications are another catch. If I apply for a simple manual job I have to play down my standard of education, because would-be-employers seem to think that if anybody with brains applies for a job that doesn't need any, there must be something wrong somewhere. Conversely, if I apply for a position that does require a good standard of education, I usually lose out to some young, upwardly mobile offcomer who possesses that magic guarantee of supreme ability, the university degree. Being a published author should help, especially in applying for jobs connected with publishing, libraries, tourism. Unfortunately it doesn't.

It is not hard to see why some people turn to crime, antisocial behaviour, and political extremism. On all sides the unemployed are beset and brainwashed by a consumer society in which they are not allowed to consume, the world of the employed and the employer. Short of living in a tent on Rockall, there is no escape from it. Read the papers, watch the TV, everywhere you are bombarded with the evidences and trappings of other people's successes. Our media drugs us, training us like Pavlov's dogs to derive our wish fulfilment from a passive voyeurism of the antics of the rich and famous. You sit and watch and read. No input is required from you.

For the unemployed there is no place beyond the fortnightly signing on at the end of a shambling queue and occasional harassment from a system which offers all the chances without any of the incentives.

The whole system is designed to exclude the unemployed as undesirables. It debases, wastes, and breeds resentment and discontent. Lives are blasted and talent is flushed down the drain.

I cry in the wilderness to that formless destiny that decrees that I should drink of this bitter cup, and wonder what I have done that I and my family should be denied the simple dignity of living a normal life. The only reply I hear are the boasts of a proud and power-drunk woman who tells me that she has improved the quality of my life. People will criticise me and shoot holes in my arguments, they will accuse me of being subjective. Perhaps they should remember it is easy to be objective when you have a job, and that their vaunted lack of bias is, like that elusive fulfilment, a luxury not available to the unemployed.

(J. Jarratt, the *Guardian*, 6 April 1989)

Jim Jarratt found himself judged and valued by his status as an unemployed person. The way in which his position was *represented* in, for example, the politician's description of unemployment and the way in which this representation was valued by other people did not match Jim Jarratt's own experience, and yet for others that representation was very real and was used by them to explain their social world. There was little that Jim Jarratt could do to influence these views. Indeed to him they seemed virtually immovable. It is important to reflect upon the way in which those representations of Jim Jarratt's circumstances formed an important part of the world he inhabited even though to him they did not accord with his own sense of his own true value.

In most respects such representations were of Jim Jarratt's position in the *public* domain. Within the *private* domain he may not have felt quite so undervalued though it is clear there are inter-connections between the public and the private. 'Arguments increase within the household, along with bitterness, anger and recriminations', he says when referring to the private domain.

Another feature of Jim Jarratt's world, which is not surprising for someone in his position, is the helplessness he felt when faced with the enormous obstacles put in his way. 'The whole system is designed to exclude the unemployed', he says. Society was seen as a 'formless destiny' over which he had virtually no control. This illustrates vividly the way in which his position as an unemployed person *structured* his ability to interact with the world. Without any explicit rules being set down he found that he was constrained in the work he could do, the private life he could lead and even in the way he was able to influence other's views of him. His relationship with the economy was thus more than just being unable to find work.

So, in terms of the questions I asked earlier, and to the extent we can generalize from one person's vivid account of his circumstances, we can see that unemployed people lack money, but much more than this. Their status and self-esteem and, perhaps more importantly, their ability to interact with the economy are substantially influenced by the fact of their unemployment. This latter point also partially answers the second question relating to the ways in which unemployment is represented. Various stereotypes of unemployment are set out in the article, which for those using them form part of their reality, and have a direct impact on the lives of the unemployed and their families.

──────────────── ACTIVITY 7 ────────────────

In Section 1.3, we made a distinction between the public and the private domain. Now, to check your understanding, see if you can write a sentence linking that distinction with Jim Jarratt's circumstances.

In Jim Jarratt's case it was his inability to gain access to work in the public domain which excluded him from the income, independence and status which many of us take for granted.

──────────────── ACTIVITY 8 ────────────────

Jim Jarratt is a white man. Limited access to the public domain is a feature of women's lives too, though work in the private domain is usually a more significant feature for women. Think back to the analysis in Block 2. Do you think Jim Jarratt's account would have been substantially different if he had been a black woman? What kind of differences and similarities would you expect to see?

Of course an answer to these questions depends on which black woman would be providing the account. There are no easy answers to my questions. Black women would be likely to experience many of the features outlined so vividly by Jim Jarratt but they would find this overlaid by other aspects of their lives relating to their gender and their race. They would, in general, be much more vulnerable than Jim Jarratt and you may recall one possible explanation which was offered in Section 4.2 of Unit 8 Part I, was the idea of the reserve army of labour. The same explanation may be appropriate for some white, working-class men. They find themselves pulled into or pushed out of work as the needs of the economy require, but for many black workers and particularly black women it can form an almost permanent feature of their lives.

SUMMARY

- Unemployment is represented in particular ways in society and unemployed people are seen as having particular characteristics. This, along with financial stringency, has a massive impact on the lives of those who are unemployed, both in the ways they are *represented* by others and the way they see themselves.

- Unemployment essentially means being cut off from active participation in the economy.

2.2   FAST FOOD

Inside the public domain there are many different kinds of work. We often think of work as typified by a male manual worker using tools such as wrenches or hammers. Alternatively, the model in one's mind's eye might be the production line for cars, or the looms and spinning machines of the textiles industry. However, these types of work are all declining in importance as a proportion of total UK employment and many more people now work in services than in manufacturing. Between 1971 and 1988, for example, the total number of employees in manufacturing industries dropped from just over 8 million to just over 5 million, whilst in the same period the numbers employed in the service sector increased from 11.6 million to 15.2 million. (Chapter 1 of the Reader refers to changing employment patterns, as you may remember, and Figure 5 graphs changes in employment from 1901.) Within the service sector organizations dealing with leisure time activities are increasingly important and within that the catering industry is a significant feature. The part of the service sector described as 'Distribution, hotels, catering and repairs' employed over 4.5 million people in 1988.

The nature of the catering industry and the products it produces have also changed so that it can act as an exemplar of changes in work organization. Traditionally, catering in high quality restaurants was a trade one entered as an apprentice or via a craft course at college. Now *fast food* — food which is served over a counter, speedily, and which can be eaten on or off the premises — is a feature of almost every high street, and the work patterns in this branch of the industry are very different from the traditional work of the chef.

To put this in context let's look briefly at the growth of the fast food industry over the last few years.

About £2.6 billion was spent on take-away food in 1987, with another £4 million on home delivery meals. This is a 12% increase on 1986, a rise which can be attributed to higher disposable incomes, declining formal family meals, and busier life styles…About 80% of British people used take-aways last year, with 20% using them at least once a week.

(*Caterer & Hotelkeeper*, 3 November 1988)

McDonald's is the biggest fast food company in the world. In 1988 world-wide sales exceeded $16 billion. The first McDonald's in the UK opened in 1974 in Woolwich and employed 60 people. In 1988 the company employed over 22,500 people in the UK and had 305 restaurants. This is a phenomenal growth but it is only part of the fast food story. In 1987 good old fish and chips were still keeping ahead of other fast foods in Britain.

Table 1   Major market segments for take-away food in Britain 1987

	sales	meals
Fish and chips	£690m	450m
Hamburgers	£410m	380m
Fried chicken	£200m	140m
Pizza	£150m	80m

Source: Fast Food Facts

This is clearly big business. Expenditure on fast food in 1987 worked out at over £30 per head or roughly one fast food meal every fortnight for every person in the country.

Whether or not we eat fast food, this is having an impact on our lives. In general, in Britain, potato growers are coming under pressure to produce the variety (Russett Burbank) which is most suitable for fast food processing, and the same influences are operating world wide for all ingredients. Kentucky Fried Chicken claimed to have nearly 6,000 outlets across the world in 1987, including the first overseas fast food restaurant in China, Pizza Hut had over 5,000 units and Taco Bell (part of the PepsiCo chain) had 2,400. British based Wimpy had 140 outlets in 21 countries.

An important point here is that these companies are best understood in terms of their global operations. Potato growers in Britain have been affected. So too

Fast food on a global scale

have beef ranches throughout the world. Thousands of square miles of the South American rain forests have been burned to provide pasture for beef cattle which can have devastating effects on the small local farmers, as well as, it is claimed, the world's ecological sub-systems.

This is the context in which we have to analyse the fast food industry — an international, competitive industry which has been experiencing considerable growth.

Working patterns in the fast food industry are typical of a process which has been seen by many observers as an important feature of capitalist forms of organization — *deskilling*. This refers to the removal of elements of skill from work so that it becomes repetitive and predictable. Such deskilling has been observed in the production line methods of large manufacturing companies but it can also be seen in other parts of the economy. For example, in carrying out research for this unit, I asked the head of one of the country's largest college departments of catering and hotel management to advise me about the way in which fast food had affected the world of catering. His first response was interesting: 'In many ways,' he said, 'it's not really catering at all — it's a branch of retailing.' What he was saying was that the craft skills of the chef had been completely removed so that to sell fast food came nearer to the job of a shop assistant than it did to the job of a chef. Why should deskilling be one of the main features of work in profit oriented organizations?

The first systematic account of this was by F.W. Taylor, in work first published in 1911. He is seen as the father of what has come to be known as *scientific management*. This set of ideas has had a major impact on the way in which work has been organized, and is based upon a mechanistic view of people at work. Essentially, workers are seen as machines. An example is often quoted of Taylor's work with a Pennsylvanian 'Deutschman' called Schmidt. Schmidt's job was to load pig iron into railway trucks. Taylor watched him and felt output could be massively increased by more efficient methods. He told Schmidt he could earn considerably more money if he did exactly as Taylor told him. Schmidt expressed an interest and Taylor then told him exactly what to do, breaking his job down into small segments and instructing him exactly when to put something down, when to pick it up, when to load it and when to rest. As a result, Schmidt's output went up by 380 per cent.

Arising from studies such as this, Taylor argued for work to be *designed* in this machine-like manner. There were a number of key principles.

- The work process had to be carefully and systematically analysed.
- The process had to be broken down into single tasks or operations.
- The tasks should be as simple as possible so that unskilled workers could perform them.

These principles result in the fragmentation of jobs and divorce the planning of work from the doing of work. Workers are thus excluded from the preparation and organization of the job which, consequently, requires very little skill or learning time (Littler, 1978). A major impact of this is the deskilling of work and an expansion in the role of management which now has to take responsibility for co-ordinating the fragmentation produced. This, in turn, means that control of work has passed substantially to the manager. A skilled worker has some autonomy over how work is carried out. A person with craft skills is essentially employed to carry out the work process which s/he has learned through an apprenticeship or similar training, and must have discretion over the precise organization of the job. Under scientific management all these decisions are taken by management who increasingly take on the function of work design and integration. Workers consequently lose much of their discretion and opportunities for decision-making.

Taylor's ideas were very influential and can be seen in operation, in particular, in factory work. They were seen as a logical, 'scientific' (hence the name) and neutral means of management which enabled simple principles to be applied to working practices. A good many work study departments were based around such principles in which everybody was seen to gain. The worker received higher wages whilst the firm improved its productivity and hence earned more profit.

Parallel to scientific management came Henry Ford's development of the assembly line. Control of the work process here is maintained through the technology itself. Management controls the flow of work but through an inanimate moving line rather than through a series of instructions. Tasks are simple and repetitive, just as in Schmidt's loading of pig iron, but the pace of the work and the precise task to be carried out are determined by the speed of the line and workers have no choice about how they carry out their jobs. As before, such mass production techniques tended to be associated with higher wages for the workers and higher profits for the company. This kind of process has come to be called, not surprisingly, *Fordism*.

It does have some problems, however. The working practices involved are extraordinarily tedious and do not produce commitment from the workers. Quality control can become a major headache for management. As a result, a number of management strategies have developed which attempt to build more responsibility back into the labour process. These include the operation of small teams of workers with overall responsibility for the product and forms of 'job enrichment' which might include a rotation of work. Essentially, management faces a dilemma. In order to remain competitive, and profitable, it must adopt techniques which maximize its return from labour. This can be done by controlling the work-force through tightly scheduled job specifications and production lines but ultimately it relies on the workers' willingness to co-operate. Thus from time to time there may be a need to encourage worker creativity and judgement. This in turn, of course, reduces control because participation of workers can only genuinely take place if there is a genuine delegation of responsibility.

———————————————— ACTIVITY 9 ————————————————

Think about the fast food industry in the light of scientific management and mass production methods. Can you see any elements of these approaches in the way fast food restaurants seem to be organized? Have a good look the next time you visit your local chip shop or hamburger bar. Does it break down the work tasks in the way Taylor might have suggested?

On first impression, fast food outlets do seem to me to break down their operations into simple repetitive tasks. Fast food is not, of course, factory work. But elements of scientific management and Fordism have affected a wide range of occupations in sectors outside manufacturing. Fast food is a rapidly expanding sector involving large international companies and a standardized product. It is highly competitive and seeks to maintain high levels of labour productivity with high profitability. How does this affect jobs?

Look at the quotations below from workers in a fast food operation (Gabriel, 1988). (Please note that Gabriel hides the identity of the company in which his research took place and these quotations should not be taken to imply any comment about any particular company.)

> It's all artificial. Pretending to offer personal service with a smile when in reality no one means it. We know this, management know this, even the customers know this, but we keep pretending. All they want to do is take

the customer's money as soon as possible. That's what it's all designed to achieve.

There are no short cuts in this job; they have perfected the best way of doing things and you have to stick to it. You just follow the rules.

I find no fulfilment at all in this job. It is convenient for me and they are helpful letting me work the hours I want, but fulfilment, satisfaction no, not here.

I have made many friends but unfortunately many of the good people here have left — the majority for better jobs. I would like to move to something more interesting, perhaps being a chef or training in electronics.

It is clear from these quotations that for the workers themselves *Taylorism* was very much part of their working lives. Remember what the main principles behind Taylorism were:

- The work process had to be carefully and systematically analysed.
- The process had to be broken down into single tasks or operations.
- The tasks should be as simple as possible so that unskilled workers could perform them.

For one worker — 'they have perfected the best way of doing things and you have to stick to it' — the work had been carefully analysed and broken down into simple tasks. Other workers, not quoted here, made similar comments and although they recognized that avoidance of the rules was sometimes possible in order to squeeze some autonomy from the system, basically all the operations were broken down into simple tasks.

Similarly these tasks were manageable by unskilled people and were not challenging — 'but fulfilment, satisfaction no, not here'. The jobs were not fulfilling though frequently the workers were too busy to be bored. Many people had left for better jobs and with unintended irony one worker wanted to look for more interesting work — 'perhaps being a chef'.

The work was not especially well paid but for many workers it was only the money which kept them at work.

So, consideration of the responses of the workers seems to confirm the impression, which I get anyway when queuing in a fast food restaurant, that scientific management principles are widespread.

———————————— ACTIVITY 10 ————————————

Why should this be so? Pause for a moment and set down the reasons you think are important for designing work in fast food according to these principles.

The key lies in the search for profits in a highly competitive international industry and the resulting pressure for the control of the work-force. The more discretion workers are able to retain the less easy it is for management to control the precise nature of the product supplied and the amount of time and resources which are involved in producing it. Fast food is highly competitive. In order to make profits firms try to control every aspect of the production process. This has the effect of creating very high rates of staff turnover — 'unfortunately many of the good people have left' — which has a training cost, though with unskilled work that training cost is low. Ultimately, however, the objective is profit and the organization will be so arranged that the highest profits possible in the circumstances are earned. 'All they want to do is take the customer's money as soon as possible. That's what it's all designed to achieve'.

In the search for profit, scientific management claims that it is a form of work design which favours neither the manager nor the worker and which enables everybody engaged in the production process to gain — from higher wages or higher profits. Each person simply performs the task to which they are most suited. Such work design is efficient in the sense that it minimizes the resources used for any particular level of output.

This view has been challenged by a number of writers with the debate centring around Harry Braverman's *Labour and Monopoly Capital* (1974) which you met briefly in Unit 7 Part I. The Braverman (or 'deskilling') thesis, which is written in the marxist tradition, starts from a different view of economic class from the Weberian hierarchical model implicit in Taylor's exposition. It takes the view that class is determined by the relationship each individual has to the means of production and, as you will recall from Block 2, this results in two broad classes of owners and workers. There is a struggle about the division of the surplus — how much workers get as wages and how much owners (usually referred to as capitalists in this thesis) get as profits. From this starting point scientific management is seen as cheapening labour by *deskilling* it, thus making transfers between different jobs easier and the ease with which any job can be filled much greater. Training time is much reduced and control is totally vested in management. Fast food firms don't want chefs therefore, according to this argument, because they possess skills which are difficult to replicate and which enable them, the chefs, to retain some control over their work. Management wish to gain control, it is claimed, because workers' interests are different from management's. In particular, the less control a worker has, the less skills are required resulting in less pay and more profits from any given level of surplus.

The important point Braverman is making here is that rationality of technique — the basic axiom of scientific management — is not neutral. It embodies within it the domination of one class, the working class, by another class, the owners, who achieve their domination through the management structures established on their behalf. Thus, he would argue, fast food workers have no autonomy and their jobs are unskilled and repetitive precisely because this structure enables the owners (through their managers) to dominate the production process and extract the maximum amount of profit (or surplus) for themselves.

It may not be surprising to anyone who has worked in a relatively menial occupation to find that management wishes to exert control over the work-force in order to increase profit. What is perhaps more difficult to grasp is the notion, put forward by Braverman, that the very structure of the work task itself is a central part of class relations with owners — or their agents — attempting to dominate and control those whom they are exploiting. This is a controversial point but it shows how deskilling can be explained from different perspectives. One view sees scientific management as a means of improving the profitability of an operation in which all can share, the other sees the organizational structure itself as a major tool by which one class dominates another.

SUMMARY

- Fast food typifies the late twentieth century as an industry with global dimensions.
- The work of chefs has been deskilled in fast food to the extent that it is no longer easily recognizable as different from many semi-skilled and unskilled retailing jobs.
- The search for profit is central to fast food operations.
- Deskilling and the control of work are a central focus of the debate about scientific management.

2.3   CLERICAL WORK

—————————————— ACTIVITY 11 ——————————————

Clerical work is something which impinges on most people's lives, either as users of organizations which undertake clerical activities — such as insurance companies, the health service or the Open University — or as employees of such organizations. What do you see as the main features of clerical work from your perspective? Write down the three main things which you see as typical of such work.

There are no right and wrong answers to this question but I think you will have considered the same features I have come up with, even if they do not figure in your final short list. The three main features for me are that clerical work seems, in general, to be relatively routine, that it is usually undertaken by women and that levels of pay are typically below the national average. These are all generalizations, of course. Not all clerical activity follows those patterns. You may have considered the Town *Clerk* as an example of clerical work, or the *Secretary* of State for Education, or in the context of the Open University, the University *Secretary*. These latter occupations are high status, have high pay and are usually undertaken by men. Indeed, they are not usually thought of as clerical work, being more commonly defined as administrative. At one time, however, to be a clerk was very highly regarded and was seen as a male occupation (and still is in some parts of the world such as India and Pakistan). Why then should clerical work in the UK — a routine job associated with less than average pay — usually be carried out by women?

The split between high status, well paid jobs and lower status, poorer paid jobs is an interesting place to start. This division has been developing since the end of the nineteenth century. Clerical work (the term originates from the work of clerics — namely monks) was originally a male preserve requiring a good education, which only men received, but the need for a clerical work-force expanded as industry and commerce expanded. Thus, in 1871, we have this fascinating argument being presented by Mr Scudamore of the Post Office about the desirability of employing female labour:

> In the first place, they have in an eminent degree the quickness of eye and ear, and the delicacy of touch, which are essential qualifications of a good operator.
>
> In the second place, they take more kindly than men or boys do to sedentary employment, and are more patient during long confinement to one place.
>
> In the third place, the wages, which will draw male operators from but an inferior class of the community, will draw female operators from a superior class.
>
> Female operators thus drawn from a superior class will, as a rule, write better than the male clerks, and spell more correctly; and, where the staff is mixed, the female clerks will raise the tone of the whole staff.
>
> They are also less disposed than men to combine for the purpose of exhorting higher wages, and this is by no means an unimportant matter.
>
> On one other ground is it especially desirable that we should extend the employment of women. Permanently established civil servants invariably expect their remuneration to increase with their years of service, and they look for this increased remuneration even in the cases, necessarily very numerous, in which from the very nature of their employment they can be of no more use or value in the twentieth

than in the fifth year of their service...Women, however, will solve these difficulties for the department by retiring for the purpose of getting married as soon as they get the chance. It is true that we do not, as the companies did, punish marriage by dismissal. It is also true that we encourage married women to return to the service; but as a rule those who marry will retire, and those only will return whose married life is less fortunate and prosperous than they had hoped.

On the whole, it may be stated without fear of contradiction that, if we place an equal number of females and males on the same ascending scale of pay, the aggregate pay to the females will always be less than the aggregate pay to the males; that, within a certain range of duty, the work will be better done by the females than by the males, because the females will be drawn from a somewhat superior class; and further, that there will always be fewer females than males on the pension list.

(Martindale, 1938)

So one set of reasons for women carrying out clerical work can be discovered in Mr Scudamore's assertions. He contended that women are more disposable than men because they will leave to get married. This had the added advantage for him that their aggregate pay will always be less than the equivalent for men. They are less disposed to combine to exhort higher wages, he says, and the work will be done better because, in general for a low average wage, they will be drawn from a somewhat superior class. From these beginnings, clerical work became the preserve of women.

'Clerical work became the preserve of women': a typing pool in 1889

The issue of skill also comes in here as in the fast food case. Mr Scudamore implies that women will be given the more routine work by his phrase 'within a certain range of duty' at the end of the quotation you have just read. Much clerical work is repetitive, though the amount of individual autonomy is usually much higher than in equivalently paid manufacturing work. The clerk can decide within limits how to carry out any given task and can structure the pattern of her or his working day.

Arguments about deskilling are more complex than in fast food however. Many clerical operations are now routinized, but alongside this standardization of working practices we can see new skills being required. As I write, in 1990, micro-computers seem to be appearing on everybody's desk. These machines are frequently used for complex activities which require training and the acquisition of new skills. For some workers, this brings greater job satisfaction and the opportunity to command higher salaries and higher status. For others, the new technology can become an imposition. Indeed the nature of clerical work, for some workers, is changing, so that they are finding themselves with less autonomy as the use of micro-processors brings the opportunity for management to exert more control over day-to-day working practices. Within the broad area of clerical work, then, we can see a number of factors in play as some work becomes more routinized at the same time as new skills become important. The new technology, however, can act as a new form of control as well as a new opportunity for some workers.

'Microcomputers seem to be appearing on everybody's desk': a VDU room in the 1980s

One issue you might reflect upon as the 'new' technology slowly ages, is the kind of gender structure which seems to be underlying its use. It is too early to have readily available statistics to draw upon, but perhaps you could observe the different ways in which men and women are employed to use modern computing resources. Is there a gender distinction between those who produce policies or develop materials to use with computers, and those who use them simply as a tool? Who decides to what use computing will be put? And who decides who will use it?

SUMMARY

- Clerical work is a major feature of modern capitalist economies and has seen considerable changes in status and working practices.
- Lower status clerical jobs are typically filled by women, who are often seen as more disposable than men and more flexible.
- Changes in skill requirements are complex, with both deskilling and reskilling occurring at the same time. Whilst this can sometimes lead to greater job satisfaction, it can also be a new form of control.

2.4   THE FUTURE OF WORK

So far in this section we have considered three different aspects of the world of work: firstly, the importance of access to the economy highlighted by the impoverished lives of those who are unemployed; secondly, the way in which the search for profits in a competitive economy can influence the nature of work organization; and, thirdly, the different jobs which are generally done by men and by women in employment. Finally, we would like you to look at some of the ideas which have been put forward in recent debates about how changes in the economy have affected the world of work. In the Reader article by Alan Warde, 'The future of work', Reader, Chapter 7, you will find a discussion which tries to assess some current and future trends in work. Warde considers arguments which claim we have moved into a world beyond Fordism and that changes in technology, products, jobs and employment contracts have resulted in a new flexibility in industrial production.

———————————— ACTIVITY 12 ————————————

In a moment you should read Warde's article. As you read it you should note down what you consider *post-Fordist* arguments have to say about the three things we have discussed in this section, namely:

- issues about who has access to the economy and what kind of access that may be, for example, part-time or full-time work, temporary or permanent employment.
- issues about the nature of work organization in a competitive world and what this has to say about the nature of skill and management control.
- issues about the kinds of jobs carried out by men and women in employment.

Note down too, Warde's comments on these arguments. Finally, as you read, consider what other important changes are being suggested in the article. We shall look at these points in more detail at the beginning of the next section.

═══════════════════ READER ═══════════════════

Now read Chapter 7 of the Course Reader.

3   WHAT IS 'REAL' WORK?

So where did your reading about the future of work leave you? Do you think work is changing? Are we about to enter a new era in which Fordist working practices are to be replaced by something else? If so, what are the consequences for us all and the work we do?

Let us start by looking at the argument that we *are* witnessing the beginning of a significant change. Those who argue we are entering into a new era of 'post-Fordism' explain it by the growth of 'flexible production methods' changing the way work is organized and therefore the type of jobs on offer and who takes them. As Warde points out, these new methods entail both 'functional flexibility' and 'numerical flexibility'. Functional flexibility is achieved by a firm employing a smaller number of workers, more in control of their own work, willing and able to do a variety of different tasks rather than a larger number of traditionally skilled workers each directed to do a particular job. The other type of flexibility is 'numerical flexibility', achieved by employing part-time, temporary or casual workers only for the times when they are needed, so that only the exact number of workers required at any point in time are employed. A post-Fordist factory may also achieve numerical flexibility by sub-contracting out irregular parts of its work to other firms; another aspect of post-Fordism is therefore the growth of smaller firms and self-employment.

Warde, you may have noted, is not entirely convinced by the argument that post-Fordism is around the corner. He agrees that many of the changes that are seen as part of the move towards flexibility are happening: the growth of small firms, of self-employment, of part-time and casual working, the increasing number of people employed in professional 'white-collar' occupations and the decline of traditional unskilled manual jobs. But he points out that these changes may have other causes. In particular, they may be due to a weakening of the power of trade unions, who have become unable to protect their members' jobs and resist increasing pressure at work. Indeed, casual and temporary work is not a new phenomenon; rather it may mark a return to the conditions of the nineteenth century. Other changes may be more an effect of the increase in women's employment as employers restructure hours in order to take advantage of the lower wages women are prepared to accept in order to get jobs which fit in with their domestic responsibilities.

Further, there is a question of the extent of these changes and where they are happening. In Britain, relatively few firms have adopted all the changes that make up the picture of the post-Fordist factory, compared with say Germany and, in particular, Japan. And even if all the advanced capitalist economies were to move in this direction, they might still rely on the Third World for the production of goods that remain suited to mass production methods.

Although the theory of post-Fordism, like that of Fordism before it, was supposed to be about manufacturing, paradoxically in Britain the shift seems to be happening more in service industries. Manufacturing is still dominated by large firms using mass production methods, while 'flexible accumulation' may be more a feature of services. It is in services that the characteristic feature of post-Fordism, the split between some well-paid professionally skilled jobs and a larger number of unskilled, insecure jobs is more apparent. If a shift to post-Fordism is happening it seems to be as part of the process known as 'deindustrialization', by which the manufacturing sector is declining as an employer relative to other sectors.

'Manufacturing is still dominated by large firms using mass production methods': a robotic production line for catalytic converters

'Flexible accumulation may be more a feature of services': a small garage

This, of course, begs the question of why theories should put so much significance on manufacturing, when it now employs less than a quarter of the workforce. One reason is perhaps some belief that manufacturing forms a sort of base upon which the rest of the economy depends and therefore that service sector jobs are in some sense not 'real jobs'. Similar views are held about other aspects of post-Fordism: Can an economy run on the basis of part-time casual employment? Are these 'real' jobs?

The next section will consider what are 'real jobs'. It will look at a range of different views of what are the characteristics a job has to have in order to be seen as the sort of work on which our economy runs. While we may all have our own notions of what constitutes a 'real job', economists have tended to look at this question in terms of how wealth is produced. For, as Warde noted at the beginning of his article, capitalist economies need to be continually changing, reorganizing their production processes, reinvesting their profits in order to bring in new methods of production. For this to be possible, wealth has to be produced in a form that can be accumulated and invested. The question economists have looked at is who are the 'productive' workers that produce the accumulable wealth upon which investment, and thus the health of the whole economy, depends.

One reason this question has excited such attention is that it has fairly immediate policy implications. If the whole economy depends on a particular sector, then it is this sector which has to be nurtured if the economy is to be kept healthy and its growth sustained. And the sort of change in policy which results from switching support from one sector to another can have far-reaching consequences even for people who are not directly employed in either sector.

You may remember that, when the Conservative government was elected in 1979, it set about implementing a policy of 'rolling back the frontiers of the state', in particular diminishing the role of the public sector in the economy in order that the 'wealth-producing' private sector be allowed to grow. The government believed that it was private industry which was productive and that the public sector, which did not produce wealth, had been effectively 'crowding-out' investment and growth in the private sector. Although they recognized that in the short term such policies would create unemployment, this was necessary in order to shake out the economy. There was no point, the government said, in creating or maintaining public sector jobs just to keep people in work because these were not 'real jobs'.

The Labour opposition on the other hand, while agreeing that public sector employment had to be paid for, did advocate employment creation through the expansion of the public sector. They saw the public sector as capable of producing wealth too; it was unemployment which was wasteful of resources. The economic theory behind these policy differences will be examined in Unit 12, but we can note here that different attitudes to where the accumulable wealth of society was created predisposed the two parties to different economic policies, policies which can make a great deal of difference to us all through their effects on unemployment, public services, state expenditure and taxation.

3.1 HISTORICAL ANTECEDENTS

Debates about what is real work have been taking place since the birth of economics in the eighteenth century. We are going to look at how two of the earliest schools of economics categorized work as either 'productive' or 'unproductive' on the basis of its contribution to the economy. Although these early theories are interesting in their own right, they are included mainly for the light they throw on more recent debates, which you will meet in the next section.

'ONLY AGRICULTURAL LABOUR IS PRODUCTIVE'

The eighteenth century French Physiocrats are often seen as the first modern economists. They introduced the idea of wealth as a surplus or, in more modern terminology, a *net product*. A net product is produced whenever output is greater than all the inputs needed to produce it.

The Physiocrats believed that only agriculture produced a net product. By using the productive powers of nature, agricultural work produced an output that was greater than the inputs necessary to produce it. This was apparent because the inputs to agriculture, the food workers consumed and the seed used on the land, were of the same type as the output produced. In manufacturing by contrast, inputs and outputs consisted of different types of things so one could not say that there was a net product, rather labour has been used to transform one type of good into another, changing its form but not producing any net increase in wealth.

This meant that for the Physiocrats the only real wealth-producing labour was agricultural. Agricultural workers are therefore referred to as 'the productive class' in contrast to 'the sterile class' of people who work in industry and commerce. While the labour of the sterile class may be useful and beneficial to society, it does not actually produce any surplus and it has therefore to be paid for from the agricultural surplus (Quesnay, 1975).

Francois Quesnay, eighteenth-century French Physiocrat

——————————————— ACTIVITY 13 ———————————————

Study Table 2 which looks at the distribution of paid workers across different types of work over the period from 1801–1951. Does this evidence, which was not of course available to the Physiocrats, support their view that all the rest of society depends on the wealth produced by agricultural workers?

Table 2   Estimated percentage distribution of the British labour force, 1801–1951 (as percentages of the total occupied population)

	Agriculture, forestry, fishing	Manufacture, mining, industry	Trade and transport	Domestic and personal	Public, professional and all other
1801	35.9	29.7	11.2	11.5	11.8
1811	33.9	30.2	11.6	11.8	19.3
1821	28.4	38.4	12.1	12.7	8.5
1831	24.5	40.8	12.4	12.6	9.5
1841	22.2	40.5	14.2	14.5	8.5
1851	21.7	40.3	15.6	13.0	5.7
1861	13.7	48.6	16.6	14.3	6.9
1871	13.1	48.1	19.5	15.3	6.8
1881	12.5	48.5	21.3	15.4	7.3
1891	10.5	48.9	22.6	15.8	7.1
1901	8.7	46.5	21.4	14.1	8.6
1911	8.3	46.4	21.5	13.9	9.9
1921	7.1	47.6	20.8	6.9	18.1
1931	6.0	45.3	22.7	7.7	18.3
1951	5.0	49.1	21.8	2.2	21.9

Source: Deane and Cole (1967) p.142

The proportion of workers in agriculture fell dramatically throughout the period covered by Table 2. Nevertheless, since the British economy was growing, we know that accumulation was taking place during nearly all that period. This does not seem to suggest that agriculture alone was producing all the wealth that was being accumulated.

Although the ideas of the Physiocrats may seem rather quaint today, two crucial ideas of theirs can be found in some later economic theories: first, the notion that unproductive workers only modify and shift around the products of productive workers, and second that it is the net product or surplus, produced by the productive workers alone, on which the whole economy has to depend.

'PRODUCTIVE LABOUR IS LABOUR EMPLOYED BY CAPITAL'

Economics proper is usually taken to have begun with the writings of Adam Smith. The title of his most famous book, *An Inquiry into the Nature and Causes of the Wealth of Nations,* published in 1776, indicates the importance to him of the question of how wealth was produced (Smith, 1904). Smith differed from the Physiocrats in his assessment of which type of labour produced a net product because he made use of the idea of the *value* of inputs and outputs of a production process, not just their physical form. This means that he recognized that inputs and outputs could be measured against each other even when they consisted of different types of things. If the value of the product was greater than the value expended in its production — both on physical inputs to the production process and on paying workers — then a net gain in value, or profit, had been made. Profits could subsequently be used to employ others, and lead to growth. But work which did not produce commodities for sale could not result in profits and was therefore necessarily unproductive:

The labour of some of the most respectable orders in the society is…unproductive of any value, and does not fix or realise itself in any permanent subject, or vendible commodity…The sovereign, for example, with all the officers both of justice and war who serve under him, the whole army and navy, are unproductive labourers. They are the servants of the public and are maintained by a part of the annual produce of the industry of other people. Their service, how honourable, how useful, or how necessary soever, produces nothing for which an equal quantity of service can afterwards be procured.

(Smith, 1904, p.369)

It was not only public employees who were not considered productive by Smith; domestic and personal servants made up a much larger group of unproductive workers throughout the nineteenth century (see Table 2). This was because, like public servants, they did not produce a product for sale. Such workers were employed not to make a profit but for the usefulness of the services they provided for their employers.

On the other hand, workers employed in capitalist enterprises were employed to make a profit and did produce a net product, which added to overall wealth. For Smith, therefore, productive labour was labour employed to make a profit.

———————————————— ACTIVITY 14 ————————————————

Do you recognize anything familiar in these ideas?

———————————————————————————————————————

They are not dissimilar from the approach of the Conservative government in 1979 we met earlier. Indeed Sir Keith Joseph, that government's first Trade and Industry minister claimed at the time that they were advocating a return to Smith's ideas by attempting to free private industry from the demands of the state and he recommended every member of his department to read Adam Smith's *Wealth of Nations*. As David Coates points out in the Traditions essay in the Reader (Chapter 22), conservative thinking on the economy in the twentieth century has been heavily influenced by liberalism.

3.2   PRODUCTIVE AND UNPRODUCTIVE LABOUR IN THE MODERN BRITISH ECONOMY

We are now going to jump more than a century to more recent times when the question of which labour is productive has again resurfaced in debates about the state of the British economy. Since the early 1970s, there has been a great deal of discussion of why the British economy has been doing less well in many respects than other advanced capitalist economies. In particular, in the 1970s growth rates of both output and productivity for the UK compared unfavourably with those of most other advanced capitalist countries.

Table 3 compares rates of growth of productivity for the seven leading industrial nations over three decades. Productivity means the output per worker and is measured by dividing total output produced by the total number of people employed in each economy. In general, economists tend to be more interested in how productivity increases, its rate of growth, than its absolute level. To work this out, the annual percentage increases in productivity are averaged over a decade to give the figures for each country in Table 3. From this we can see that in the 1970s all countries experienced lower productivity growth than they had in the 1960s, but the rate for the UK was particularly low, the lowest of all except for the US. The question was why was this happening, what was different about the British economy and what could be done about it.

Table 3   Output per person employed for seven leading industrial nations

Whole economy	Average annual % changes		
	1960–70	1970–80	1980–88
UK	2.4	1.3	2.5
US	2.0	0.4	1.2
Japan	8.9	3.8	2.9
Germany	4.4	2.8	1.8
France	4.6	2.8	2.0
Italy	6.3	2.6	2.0
Canada	2.4	1.5	1.4
Average	3.5	1.7	1.8

Source: UK data from Central Statistical office. Other countries' data from OECD and national GNP or GDP figures reprinted from Treasury (1989)

A number of different economists gave similar answers which rested on a claim that the key to economic growth and prosperity lay in a productive core of the economy; the problems of the British economy had arisen because this productive core was being dragged down by the unproductive demands of the rest of the economy. But the economists differed in their ideas about where to locate this productive core and therefore they also disagreed about the appropriate remedy.

'MANUFACTURING IS THE KEY TO GROWTH'

One view of where the productive core lay was put forward by the Cambridge economist, Nicolas Kaldor, who was an adviser to the Labour government of 1964–70. He believed that manufacturing provided the motor of growth for the economy, because the productivity of work in manufacturing was subject to continual increases through the use of larger plants and the introduction of technological improvements. When productivity in manufacturing increased so that the same output could be produced by fewer workers, the remainder could be freed to provide for further expansion either in the same plant or elsewhere. But the productivity of service workers could not be increased in the same way, because the provision of a service often relied on it taking a particular personal form. Whereas, for example, the number of people needed to produce a motor car was continually declining through technological improvements, the number of people needed to teach a class of children remained much the same (Kaldor, 1966).

Agricultural work was similar to manufacturing in that its productivity could be increased by technological improvements. But agriculture was inherently limited in the contribution it could make to the economy by its need for land which was in fixed supply. Unlike manufacturing, whose possibilities for growth were limitless, British agriculture would always be constrained by the quantity of land available. Productivity increases therefore resulted in falling agricultural employment as fewer workers were needed to work each acre. It was only manufacturing which, in the right conditions, could show growth over a long period in both productivity and employment.

ACTIVITY 15

Do Kaldor's views remind you of any of the older theories of productive and unproductive labour you met in the previous section?

Kaldor's views were similar to those of the Physiocrats in that they both saw particular sectors of work as productive. However, they differed not only in which sectors they chose but also in their reasons for choosing them. For the Physiocrats, because of nature's productive powers agricultural work alone was productive and the rest of the economy depended for food on the surplus it produced. For Kaldor, by contrast, manufacturing constituted the productive core because the growth of the rest of the economy depended on manufacturing's potential for productivity increases.

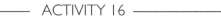

—————————————————— ACTIVITY 16 ——————————————————

In order to assess Kaldor's theory of how economic growth is encouraged, think which of the following statements of his theory are borne out by what you have read so far in this Unit.

1   Services are not subject to technological increases in productivity.

2   Productivity increases have led to falling employment in agriculture.

3   It is growth in manufacturing employment which explains the growth of the economy as a whole until the 1960s.

---

1   In Section 2, fast food was given as an example of a service which has been organized along similar lines to manufacturing in pursuit of increased productivity. Similarly, clerical work, another service, has been transformed by the advent of new technology in recent years.

2   Table 2 showed how the percentage of workers employed in agriculture in Britain has fallen since 1801. We cannot determine the cause of this fall from such figures, but it must have meant that agricultural workers were available in large numbers throughout the nineteenth century to take jobs in manufacturing and services. By the beginning of the twentieth century the share of agricultural employment was falling more slowly and can no longer be seen as the main source of new workers for other parts of the economy; the decline of domestic service looks more significant for the first half of this century.

3   Using Table 2 again, throughout the nineteenth century and first half of the twentieth, the percentage of workers employed in manufacturing was rising. Indeed, the only period in which manufacturing employment fell significantly as a share of total employment was the depressed 1920s — giving some support to the view that manufacturing employment is a significant factor in the growth of the economy. But, again, causes cannot be determined from the figures alone, the share of employment in trade and transport has risen throughout the period too; but this must surely be an effect of a growing economy rather than its cause.

—————————————————— ACTIVITY 17 ——————————————————

Now look at Figure 1 to see whether more recent evidence supports Kaldor's view.

Figure 1 shows quite a different picture for the 1970s. Manufacturing employment declined from its peak of nearly eight million in 1966 to just about six million in 1979. Over the same period service employment increased by about the same amount. This could be seen to lend some support to Kaldor's view that the problems of the 1970s stemmed from service employment squeezing the manufacturing core and thus rendering it incapable of providing the productivity increases necessary for growth.

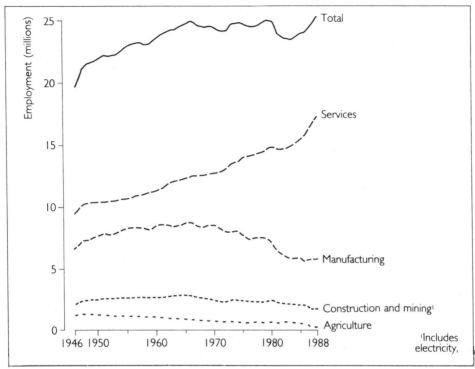

Figure 1   Employment by sector in the UK, 1946–88
Source: data from Ministry of Labour and Department of Employment

Kaldor's view was that a growing manufacturing base was needed to provide the productivity increases upon which the growth and prosperity of the rest of the economy depended. The decline in manufacturing employment would not have necessarily mattered if the productivity of the workers remaining in manufacturing was increasing fast enough so that the sector's overall output was growing strongly. But that clearly was not the case in the 1970s. From

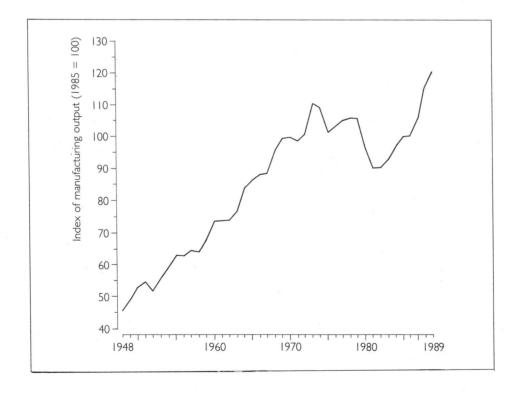

Figure 2   Manufacturing output, United Kingdom, 1948–89
Source: Treasury, 1987

Figure 2 it can be seen that manufacturing output fell sharply in the recessions of 1973–4 and 1979–81 and recovered only weakly in between. Further, Figure 3 shows that manufacturing productivity grew very slowly and unevenly in the 1970s compared with previous periods.

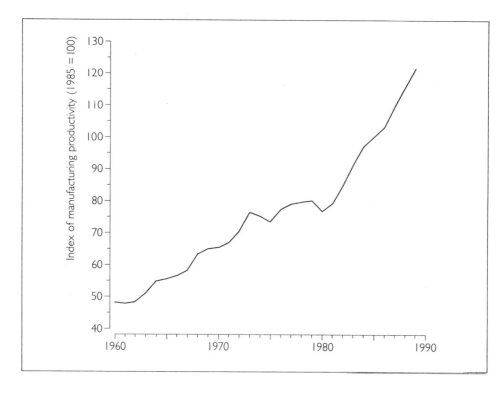

Figure 3   Manufacturing productivity 1960–89
Source: Department of Employment (1990)

Figures 1 and 2 give a somewhat different picture for the 1980s. Manufacturing employment continued to fall but output began to rise after 1982, though it took until 1988 to recover its 1973 level. Further, Figure 3 shows that manufacturing productivity did rise sharply in the 1980s, suggesting again that there might be something in Kaldor's view that a growing manufacturing sector was what mattered. But, although output was growing in manufacturing in the 1980s, employment continued to fall. Perhaps manufacturing was beginning to function like agriculture had before with productivity increases resulting in lower employment in the sector. If this continues then the only expanding sector of employment will be services, an outcome that would have worried Kaldor a great deal.

Would he have been right to worry about the growth of service employment? That there has been a significant shift in employment from manufacturing to services over the past twenty five years is not in dispute. However, the view that increasing service employment is a problem for an economy can be, and has been challenged. Indeed, many people would argue that, rather than being the symptom of any problem, it is the mark of a well developed economy that a large number of people can be employed in providing services for the rest of the community. Similar trends have indeed been evident in all other advanced capitalist countries without leading to the problems of the British economy.

However, disputes about the desirability of services do not really challenge Kaldor's view that services could not provide the basis for growth because they were not subject to significant productivity increases. Are services really so different? Does not the introduction of new technology into service industries throw into doubt the idea that productivity improvements are impossible there?

—————————————————— ACTIVITY 18 ——————————————————

Turn back to Table 3. What does this tell us about productivity growth for the UK in the 1980s in comparison with:

(a) previous years, and

(b) other advanced capitalist countries?

Taking the decade as a whole, UK productivity growth was much higher in the 1980s than in the 1970s, and even slightly higher than in the 1960s, suggesting that growing service employment had not eroded the basis for productivity increases. It was even doing relatively well compared with most other countries, whose rates of productivity growth were continuing to fall as they had in the 1970s.

However, when we look at the figures for the 1980s in more detail, we find they do not give quite such a clear-cut picture. Table 4 gives annual productivity increases for each year up to 1988, the last year for which data was available when this course was written. From this it can be seen that the 1980s were a very mixed decade. In 1980 the economy was in recession and in this year there was a productivity fall. As one might expect, in the following few years when the economy was shaking itself out of that recession, productivity growth was high. But then it slowed down and fell again in 1988 to below the average for the leading industrial nations. As I write now in 1990, it is not clear what the trend will be for the UK productivity in the 1990s.

Table 4   Output per person employed

UK	Annual % changes
1980	−2.2
1981	2.2
1982	4.3
1983	4.3
1984	0.9
1985	2.0
1986	2.4
1987	2.7
1988	1.5

Source: Central Statistical Office

'THE STRENGTH OF THE ECONOMY DEPENDS ON ITS MARKETED OUTPUT'

Another explanation at the time of the relatively poor performance of the British economy was put forward by the Oxford economists Robert Bacon and Walter Eltis. They also explained it by a shortage of productive workers, but drew a different distinction between the productive and unproductive work. Arguing against Kaldor's view that service work was 'unproductive' this is how they put their view:

> Instead of dividing economic activities into those that are *industrial* and those that are *non-industrial* they can be divided instead between those that produce *marketed* output and those which do not. Almost everything that industry produces is *marketed*, that is, it is sold to someone. The private-sector services are sold, so they are *marketed*. Defence, on the other hand, is not marketed; no one pays for the use of a regiment or frigate. What the National Health Service provides, and most schools, is also not marketed, and the services provided by policemen and civil servants are not marketed; so they must spend their incomes on the marketed products of the rest of the community...

All exports are marketed, so the economy's entire exports of goods and services must be drawn from the economy's total pool of marketed output. All investment is marketed so this must also come from the economy's total marketed output. Finally, all money that workers, salary earners and pensioners spend must necessarily go to buy marketed output. *Hence the marketed output of industry and services taken together must supply the total private consumption, investment and export needs of the whole nation.*

(Bacon and Eltis, 1976, pp.26–7, emphasis in original)

—————————————— ACTIVITY 19 ——————————————

Does this position on the distinction between productive and unproductive labour remind you of any of the views discussed earlier?

Bacon and Eltis's distinction is effectively the same as Smith's. The difference in the way they put their views reflects a shift, in the two hundred years that separates these authors, in the composition of the 'unproductive' workforce. In Smith's time it largely consisted of personal servants and so state employees were seen similarly as civil or military servants. By the 1970s the state was involved in a far wider range of economic activities and differentiating between those had become much more important.

As we have seen, the Conservative government of 1979 claimed Adam Smith as one of its mentors and in practice its policies were ones that were consistent with the views of Bacon and Eltis. However its public pronouncements often took a slightly different position, classifying all public sector production as unproductive. This is how Mrs. Thatcher put it:

> The private sector creates the goods and services we need both to export to pay for our imports and the revenue to finance public services. So one must not overload it. Every man (sic) switched away from industry and into government will reduce the productive sector and increase the burden on it at the same time.
>
> (*ibid*, p.32)

But the distinction drawn by Bacon and Eltis was not just between public and private sectors, between a sector financed and run by the state, and one owned and controlled by private capital:

> It must be emphasised that the distinction between the market and non-market sectors of the economy is not the same as the distinction between the public and private sectors. A profit-making nationalised industry is in the public sector but its entire output is marketed. Council houses, if they are let at rents which cover all costs, also provide much-desired marketed output. It is only in so far as nationalised industries make losses and houses are let at rents which fail to cover costs that they are part of the non-market sector which has to draw on the market sector for its consumption and investment requirements. In reality much of nationalised industry makes a loss, and council house rents cover only a fraction of costs, so perhaps half the amount spent on them is non-market expenditure.
>
> (*ibid*, pp.29–30)

————————————— ACTIVITY 20 —————————————

Look at Table 5 which shows the composition of the workforce in employment in the first ten years after Mrs Thatcher's government came to power in 1979. Do you think that government could claim in 1989 that it had been successful in easing the burden of the unproductive on the productive sector of the economy? And what do you think Bacon and Eltis would have said about the government's record?

Table 5   UK public sector and private employment (at mid-year thousands of persons)

	Central government	Local authorities	Total central and local government	Public corporations	Total public sector	Private sector	Work-related government training programmes[1]	Total workforce in employment
1979	2 387	2 997	5 384	2 065	7 449	17 944	—	25 393
1980	2 393	2 956	5 349	2 038	7 387	17 940	—	25 327
1981	2 419	2 899	5 318	1 867	7 185	17 161	—	24 346
1982	2 400	2 865	5 265	1 756	7 021	16 887	—	23 908
1983	2 384	2 906	5 290	1 662	6 952	16 658	16	23 626
1984	2 359	2 942	5 301	1 610	6 911	17 149	175	24 235
1985	2 360	2 958	5 318	1 261	6 579	17 780	176	24 618
1986	2 337	3 010	5 347	1 199	6 546	17 789	226	24 756
1987	2 312	3 062	5 374	996	6 370	18 393	311	25 306
1988	2 322	3 081	5 403	924	6 327	19 200	343	25 749
1989	2 303	2 934	5 237	844	6 081	19 782	466	26 329

[1]   Participants in the YTS who receive work experience, participants in the new JTS and some trainees on similar Northern Ireland schemes. Those with contracts of employment are included in the appropriate employment category, but others cannot be split between those in public sector workplaces and those in private sector workplace.

The government was successful in reducing public sector employment. However, it did this almost entirely by privatizing the profitable nationalized industries. Since these already produced marketed products, privatization by itself made no difference as to whether the workers in them would be considered productive by Bacon and Eltis. You should check yourself what the effect on the marketed sector as a whole was by adding the row labelled 'Public corporations' to that labelled 'Private sector'.

Mrs Thatcher's view of the public sector as a burden on private industry did not depend solely on arguments concerning which sector is productive. She also had objections to the state running industry as an unnecessary expansion of its role and an undesirable interference in personal freedom. Nevertheless, her government's policies did take note of the distinctions Bacon and Eltis drew. For, although it privatized wherever possible, the government also tried to make the remaining industries in the public sector profitable, or, as Bacon and Eltis would say, to turn as large a proportion of their output as possible into marketed output. In practice, of course, this meant to run them as much as possible as if they *were* private sector industries.

Bacon and Eltis claim that to make a distinction between productive and unproductive labour does not have to mean that we should see the former as more desirable in itself. Indeed, as they point out, it may be the other way round:

> It must be emphasised that almost all the civilised activities of a modern society are wholly or largely non-marketed. Both Covent Garden and Glyndebourne cover only a fraction of their costs by selling tickets, and universities, schools, art galleries, libraries and hospitals produce outputs which are almost entirely non-marketed. Defence is

also non-marketed so, in times of war, countries perforce vastly increase the non-market sector of their economies. It can almost be said that a country with a larger non-market sector than another similar country will be either militarily stronger or more civilised, but it must be able to afford to maintain its large non-market sector.

(*ibid*, p.31)

Further a recognition that the unproductive sector has to be paid for does not necessarily lead to a particular policy prescription. A choice can be made between cutting down the non-marketed sector or allowing it to grow but accepting the costs of financing it from the marketed sector, that is, from private consumption. Such a course has been taken in Sweden, Norway and Denmark where a greater shift towards public services, the non-marketed sector, has taken place than in Britain. Provided there is the political will to pay for this choice it is perfectly viable economically. These authors claim to put no particular moral or political worth on their notion of productive labour; however they insist, like previous economists, that the unproductive sector has to be built on the basis of, and paid for by, the productive sector.

This claim has been criticized as disingenuous for, in practice, terms like 'productive' and 'unproductive' do seem to carry some moral implications. Bacon and Eltis have also been criticized for ignoring the importance of much non-market work. Their statement that the market sector has to pay for the non-market sector ignores the dependence that runs in the other direction. Much work that produces no marketed outcome is not only more 'civilized' than market-oriented work; it is also essential for the marketed sector to continue. It is the content of work, not just whether it can be sold that is important to the health of the economy. For example, workers have to be healthy if they are to work well. Privatizing the health service will have the short-term effect of reducing the 'burden' of the non-market sector on the marketed output of the economy. But if workers do not get adequate health care from a privatized health care system, if they cannot afford it, for example, then the long-run effect may be not only a weaker and less healthy population, but the output of the market sector itself may suffer.

SUMMARY

- Nicolas Kaldor and Bacon and Eltis tried to explain the poor growth of the British economy by the increasing demands a growing unproductive sector was making on a declining number of productive workers.

- Their theories differ as to which work is seen as productive and why. Kaldor saw manufacturing as the source of productivity increases and therefore of growth in the economy as a whole. Bacon and Eltis saw the non-market sector as having to be paid for out of the production of the market sector.

- Each theory leads to its own policy prescription to encourage growth: Kaldor would encourage manufacturing whereas Bacon and Eltis would advocate that as much output as possible should be produced in a marketable form.

- This is not the only policy alternative; retaining or expanding the number of unproductive workers may be considered desirable, but this has to be paid for. For Kaldor, if services expand growth has to slow down, whereas for Bacon and Eltis non-marketed production has to be paid for from private consumption.

3.3   WHAT IS REAL WORK? PUBLIC AND PRIVATE AGAIN

In ordinary speech we also distinguish between different types of jobs, when we say things such as 'I'm not properly back at work yet, I'm just working part-time' or 'She hasn't got a proper job yet, just a temporary one'. It was these sort of distinctions that lay behind the question of whether the part-time, temporary and casual jobs being created by the search for numerical flexibility were really 'proper' jobs. Such distinctions turn on the meaning of the job not for the economy, but for the person doing it.

These questions are similar to those we considered in the first section of this unit when we looked at the differences between work in the public and private domains. There we noted that one reason why work in the private domain, however important it is to society, tends to go unrecognized is because it brings in no money to the person doing it. The distinction between paid and unpaid work is not however a total divide.

─────────────── ACTIVITY 21 ───────────────

Look at Table 6 below which shows the employment status of people in employment for March 1989.

1   Which sex is a part-time employee most likely to be?

2   Which sort of job is a woman most likely to have?

Table 6   Part-time and full-time employment of men and women

March 1989	Numbers employed		Total employed (thousands)
	Full-time	Part-time	
All	16 629	5 184	21 813
Men	10 769	901	11 670
Women	5 860	4 283	10 143

Source: Department of Employment

The vast majority of part-time employees are women. However, more women are employed full-time than part-time. So while the typical part-time employee is a woman, the typical woman employee does not work part-time. This discrepancy arises from the varied employment histories of women, reflecting not only different patterns among different ethnic groups, but also the different demands made on women at different stages of their lives by the needs of children (see Table 7), elderly relatives and other domestic commitments.

Table 7   Part-time and full-time employment of women with and without dependent children

Spring 1987	Numbers employed		Total employed* (thousands)
	Full-time	Part-time	
Women with youngest dependent child:			
Under 5 years	299	697	1 000
5 to 9 years	255	731	988
10 to 15 years	487	865	1 354
Women without dependent children under 16 years	4 603	2 317	6 952
All women	5634	4610	10 294

Employees and self-employed including those on government training schemes.

*Includes those who did not state whether they were employed full-time or part-time.

Source: CSO, 1990, p.72

Nevertheless, a part-time employee is more likely to be a woman than a man and this reflects the structural inequalities in men's and women's roles with respect to work in the private domain. To view only full-time employment as proper work, therefore, ignores the contribution many women make to the economy and is increasingly becoming an outdated picture. Similarly, promotion by seniority and such rules as 'last-in-first-out' to decide who should be made redundant are based on valuing a typically male pattern of uninterrupted employment over many women's more interrupted and varied careers. To see only one pattern of employment as normal is unrealistic and tends to devalue both women's work in the private domain and their considerable contribution to the economy through their paid employment.

Further, work in the private domain does not produce a product for the market; this, as we saw in Section 1 of this unit, is another reason why it is sometimes not counted as proper work. There we defined another meaning of 'work' as activity which contributes to the reproduction of society. The contribution of such work to the creation of wealth in the economy tends to go unrecognized not only in popular discourse, but also in the theories of economists. In particular those, such as Bacon and Eltis, who claim that paid employment creates wealth if it produces products for sale must, by the same argument, not count work in the private domain as wealth creating.

In practice, *all* the different economic theories we have looked at so far have concentrated on work in the public domain alone; the problems of the private domain, like the work done in it, have been invisible. As a result, in assessing the policy options developed from such theories, the effects on work and workers in the private domain are largely ignored. Given that there are invisible costs and difficulties in implementing any policy, those borne by workers in the private domain will be invisible compared with the costs imposed on those who do the 'real work' recognized by economic theory. For example, cutbacks in state provision of welfare services, such as day-care for the elderly or children, may mean a transfer of some of the work done to workers employed by private firms, but, in many cases, will simply mean that more work is done unpaid in the private domain.

This concentration on production for the market and paid employment has been criticized by feminist writers who want policy to be informed by a broader conception of work to include both production and reproduction. This is how Anna Coote and Beatrix Campbell put it:

> Patriarchal politics — whether on the left, centre or right — has a distorted perspective. Its analyses of what is wrong and how things work in society, as well as its objectives, begin from and are focussed upon one relatively limited area of life: production. As women, we assert a different approach to politics, which has a double axis: reproduction and production. This embraces domestic work as well as paid work, relations within the family and community as well as relations between labour and capital.
>
> (Coote and Campbell, 1982, pp.241–2)

But if this approach were successful a very different meaning would have to be put on the idea of 'work', in which the distinctions between private and public would cease to have the same structuring importance that they have today. And this in turn would mean we would be living in a very different sort of economy.

> ## SUMMARY
>
> - Popular conceptions of what is real work often turn on what it means to the person doing it and exclude work which is not paid.
> - Economic theories and the policies developed from them also tend to ignore work in the private domain.
> - But such work contributes to the reproduction of society and hence is essential to the creation of wealth within it.

CONCLUSION

In this unit, we have been exploring the meaning and importance of work in our society. We found that the distinction between public and private domains was a crucial one in defining what was meant by work, who does it and what recognition they get for it.

For work, exchange marks the critical boundary between public and private domains, and for some economic theories between productive and unproductive work. In a capitalist economy, much work is done in exchange for a wage and most products are bought and sold on the market. The market, both for labour and for products, is therefore a crucial feature of such economies. Following on from this, the next unit will explore different views of the market and how it functions in a capitalist economy like ours.

REFERENCES

Anderson, J. and Ricci, M. (eds) (1990) *Society and Social Science: a Reader,* Milton Keynes, The Open University.

Bacon, R. and Eltis, W. (1976) *Britain's Economic Problem: Too Few Producers,* London, Macmillan.

Braverman, H. (1974) *Labour and Monopoly Capital,* New York, Monthly Review Press.

Central Statistical Office (1990) *Social Trends 1989,* London, HMSO.

Coote, A. and Campbell, B. (1982) *Sweet Freedom: the Struggle for Women's Liberation,* London, Pan Books.

Deane, P. and Cole, W.A. (1967) *British Economic Growth 1688–1959,* Cambridge, Cambridge University Press.

Department of Employment (1990) *Annual Supplement.*

Gabriel, Y. (1988) *Working Lives in Catering,* London, Routledge & Kegan Paul.

HM Treasury (1989) *Economic Progress Report,* April, HMSO.

Jarratt, J. (1989) 'Government surplus', *The Guardian,* Thursday, 6 April.

Kaldor, N. (1966) *Causes of the Slow Rate of Growth of the United Kingdom* (inaugural lecture) Cambridge, Cambridge University Press.

Littler, C.R. (1978) 'Understanding Taylorism', *British Journal of Sociology,* vol. 29.

Martindale, H. (1938) *Women Servants of the State 1870–1938: A History of Women in the Civil Service,* London, George Allen & Unwin.

Quesnay, F. (1975) 'Reply to the Report by M.H. on the advantages of industry and commerce and on the fecundity of the so-called sterile class' (first published 1766) translated in C. Napoleoni, *Smith, Ricardo, Marx,* Oxford, Blackwell.

Smith, A. (1904) *An Inquiry into the Nature and Causes of the Wealth of Nations* London, Grant Richards. (First published in 1766.)

Taylor, F.W. (1972) 'The principles of scientific management' in Davis, L.E. and Taylor, J.C. (eds) *Design of Jobs,* Penguin. (Article first published in 1911.)

ACKNOWLEDGEMENTS

Grateful acknowledgement is made to the following sources for permission to reproduce material in this unit:

Text

Jarrett, J. 'Government Surplus', *The Guardian* 6 April 1989.

Figures

Figures 1 and 2: Allen, J. and Massey, D.(eds) (1989) *The Economy In Question,* Sage/The Open University; *Figure 3*: Oulton, N. 'Productivity Growth in Manufacturing' from National Institute of Economic and Social Research (1989) *National Institute Economic Review.*

Tables

Table 1: Lobstein, T. Carruthers, F. Kirman, M. R. (1988) *Fast Food Facts,* Camden Press; *Table 2*: Deane, P. and Cole, W. A. (1967) *British Economic Growth 1688–1959,* Cambridge University Press; Table 7: *Social Trends 1989,* by permission of the Controller of Her Majesty's Stationery Office.

Photographs

p. 9: Monique Cabral/Format; *p. 12*: National Children's Home/John R. Simmons; *p. 14*; Greater London Photographic Library; *p. 20*: Denis Thorpe/ The Guardian; *p. 23*; J. P. Laffont/Sygma; *p. 29*: Mary Evans Picture Library; *p. 30*: Jenny Matthews p. 30/ZFormat; *p. 32* (left): General Motors; *p. 32* (right): Brenda Prince/Format; *p. 34*: Mansell Collection.

UNIT 11   COMPETITIVE MARKETS

Prepared for the Course Team by Vivienne Brown

CONTENTS

1   INTRODUCTION

The 1980s was a period of renewed belief in 'economic liberalism', but more recently some of the old doubts about the merits of free markets have begun to find a wider hearing again. The post-war period from 1945 to the end of the 1970s had come to be associated at the policy level with an excessive level of 'interference' by the state in the workings of the economy. High levels of public expenditure, high taxes, excessive trades union power and an overbearing 'nanny state' were thought to be the signs and symbols that the balance between market activity and state involvement had somehow got out of hand. During the 1980s there was a reaction against state involvement in the economy, and a celebration of the role of markets in organizing economic activities. The buzz words of this decade were privatization, deregulation and market testing. Governments in many different countries sought to roll back the boundaries of the state and tried to introduce the financial disciplines of the market in hitherto state-regulated areas of economic life.

In the UK, this revival of economic liberalism is associated with the policies introduced by Prime Minister Margaret Thatcher's administrations following her first election victory in 1979, but this trend towards economic liberalism was evident around the globe. In the United States, it was associated with President Ronald Reagan and his emphasis on reducing taxation and establishing supply-side incentives. In the then USSR, it was associated with Mr Mikhail Gorbachev's policy of *perestroika* and *glasnost* introduced in 1985, but even these momentous reforms soon came to be seen as too tentative and so were replaced in Russia by the more stringent market policies of President Boris Yeltsin. In New Zealand, Prime Minister David Lange introduced deregulation, public sector reform and privatization, and these policies were extended by later governments to include cutbacks on the welfare state. In Europe, these ideas could be seen behind some aspects of the move towards European integration, in particular, behind the move towards setting up the single European market by the end of 1992.

By the mid-1990s, however, some of this market-led euphoria was beginning to evaporate. High rates of growth had been achieved during some of the years of the 1980s, but recession was again taking its toll in Western Europe with high interest rates and soaring unemployment rates. This time around, it was not only the unskilled and poorly educated who felt the recession annihilate their income and lifestyle. For the first time, the highly prosperous beneficiaries of the market-led boom years, the Yuppies themselves, had to learn the lessons of recession and take their turn in the dole queue. The high levels of debt incurred during the boom years of easy credit and inflated property values, now came to form a millstone around the necks of ordinary consumers. Now they had to retrench on their expenditure and start to pay the price for the heady consumerism of the earlier years.

In Eastern Europe, too, the excitement of the dissolution of the political power of communism gave way to the daunting realities of the wholesale transformation of economic life. Political freedom and economic freedom went hand in hand, it was thought, but the process of constructing a market-based economy raised complex questions about the nature of economic freedom and the kinds of institutional frameworks and cultural assumptions that need to be in place before a successful market economy can develop. The painful reverberations of this process were also felt abroad as the costs of German reunification resulted in high interest rates and a tough monetary environment at a time of economic recession.

With the 1990s, then, there emerged in some quarters a more dispassionate attempt to evaluate the benefits and the losses involved in the move to more market-led economic systems. With the old polarization between capitalism and communism seen as a thing of the past, it came to be realized afresh that there are inevitably costs as well as benefits arising from the untrammelled power of competitive markets. It also came to be realized again that 'competitive markets' are themselves highly diverse and depend very much on the kinds of goods produced and the types of institutional frameworks in which they have to operate.

In this unit we shall look at some of the benefits and costs of competitive markets. In doing this we shall find that the debate here links up very closely with the ongoing debate between liberalism and social reformism within the traditions of social thought. This debate has been going on for a long time as you will appreciate from Chapter 22 in the Course Reader. Liberalism has always extolled the benefits of competitive markets whereas social reformism tries to ameliorate what it sees as the harsh and unacceptable consequences of market capitalism. At the moment both these traditions are also having to take on board the lessons of the 1980s experiment with economic liberalism as well as the current economic experiences of the formerly communist countries of Russia and Eastern Europe.

This debate about the role of competitive markets also links with the course theme of 'representations and reality'. What we shall find is that there is more than one way of conceptualizing the notion of a 'competitive market', and that these differences in turn feed into policy debates. In Unit 9 you met the notion of 'contested concepts'. There you learnt that some social science concepts are interpreted in a number of different ways, and that these different interpretations lead to debate and arguments. In this unit, we shall find that the notion of 'competition' can be thought of as a contested concept, where writers from different theoretical positions try to argue for the greater relevance of their own particular meaning of the term.

In the course of this unit, I hope you will come to understand:

1 How the debate about markets is central to the ongoing debate between liberalism and social reformism.

2 What is meant by the term 'competitive markets' and why there is more than one interpretation of this term.

3 Some of the advantages and disadvantages of markets.

4 How these debates about the market provide yet another example of the course theme 'representation and reality'.

2 COMPETITIVE MARKETS AND THE LIBERAL TRADITION

On 5 February 1989, Sky Television was first beamed into 600,000 homes in the UK and Eire via satellite dish aerials or cable television, and a jubilant Mr Rupert Murdoch, Chairman of News International Limited the majority share-holder in Sky Television, proclaimed that: 'Sky Television will bring competition, choice and quality to British Television. The monopoly is broken' (*The Times*, 6 February 1989).

Mr Murdoch's claim here represents what is perhaps a familiar understanding of markets. Left unhindered, different suppliers compete against each other in offering the consumer a reliable and attractive product at a reasonable price.

Competition promotes 'choice and quality' and very often, it is thought, lower prices too. Here competition is contrasted with monopoly, its opposite, where producers who are protected from competition become inefficient and do not provide choice, quality or low price for the consumer.

Just how competitive television may become over the next decade or so is something we shall have to wait to see. It is worth noting though that the event being celebrated by Mr Murdoch here was the increase in the number of suppliers by one; his own Sky Television. Also note that until British Satellite Broadcasting launched their own satellite service in 1990, Sky Television had a true monopoly of satellite broadcasting as it was the one and only supplier. In the event, BSB itself traded independently only for a short period of time and very soon merged with Sky Television.

These details suggest that we should be wary when we read striking claims in the newspapers about 'competition' since this term (as we shall see later) is open to different meanings. But what Mr Murdoch's statement does illustrate is the commitment to competitive markets that can be traced back to the origins of the liberal tradition and the writings of Adam Smith in *The Wealth of Nations* in the eighteenth century.

But in all this talk of competitive markets, just what do we mean by a 'market'? This is a term used all the time by economists but their use of it is probably not the same as the one we recognize in everyday speech. Normally, in everyday language, a market is the name we give to a site where goods are sold on open stalls or in small boutiques. Many of these market sites are of long historical origin as markets and fairs have been held there for years, sometimes centuries. The local open air market selling fruit, vegetables, household goods, bric-à-brac and clothing is the modern descendant of these older markets. Petticoat Lane in the East End of London is a well known example of such open air street markets in the UK where many a bargain can be found. Most towns have a covered market, too, comprising stalls and small shops selling largely greengroceries, groceries and household goods. Antique markets are also common as traders cash in on the national 'heritage' industry.

In these examples, the term market refers to a physical site where goods are bought and sold. Very often, though, we talk about the market for a commodity in a more general sense that is not restricted to a specific venue where buyers and sellers meet together. We might talk about the market for television sets, for example, or the world tin market, meaning the conditions under which television sets or tin generally are being bought and sold. Alternatively, we might specify something about the boundaries of the market in terms of geographical areas. We might refer to the case of the French butter market or the American market for beefburgers, but this would still be a very general notion of a market and doesn't refer to any particular physical place where traders and customers meet.

The goods traded here are all tangible goods in a physical sense, but we could just as well refer to intangible goods or 'services', such as the market for house loans or for haircuts. We could also refer to the market for different labour skills, such as the market for welders or the market for opticians. We could even talk about the market for labour, in general terms, without having to specify labour skills.

In economics writings, however, we also use the term market in an even more general sense to refer to the whole process of buying and selling goods and services. When we talk about the role of markets in organizing economic life or the characteristics of a market-based system, it is this more general meaning which is being used. There is an underlying assumption that most labour, goods and services are traded in markets so that most forms of production and consumption are mediated through acts of buying and selling. In the previous unit you studied the world of work and the economy. There the world of paid work was contrasted with the domain of unpaid work. In economists' language, it is paid work that is channelled through the market, a labour market, while unpaid work is not. Thus, in the language of Unit 10, much of the public domain corresponds to activities that are coordinated by the market. In this more general usage, references to the role of markets refer not to this or that market, but to the general ways in which an interrelated system of markets serves to coordinate a society's production and consumption decisions.

It is this more general meaning that is the subject of this unit. How do competitive markets in general work, and what are their advantages and disadvantages? This aspect of economics is sometimes referred to as 'microeconomics' in that it is based on analyses of how individual markets for particular commodities (or 'markets in the small') — actually function and interrelate. (This is in contrast with 'macroeconomics' which analyses the entire aggregate economy — or 'markets in the large'.) Liberalism as a broad tradition of thought has always stressed the view that competitive markets promote 'efficiency' and that the consumer will benefit from this. There are different aspects to the notion of economic efficiency, but in essence it means that competition amongst suppliers will ensure that consumers ultimately get the best deal: goods are produced most efficiently at minimum cost without wastage in order to meet customer requirements. Further, liberalism has also stressed that free market outcomes embody principles of justice in that each person receives the full reward for their own economic services or property.

This optimistic view of a market-based society has been a key ingredient of liberalism, and it has proved immensely powerful. A brief summary of the liberal tradition of thought was provided in Unit 5, Section 2.1, and a more detailed account of its historical development is outlined in Chapter 22 of the Course Reader. This would be a good time to read Section 2.1 of the Traditions Essay if you have not already done so.

<hr>

READER

Now read Section 2.1 of Chapter 22 and note in particular what it says about the 'market' in the sub-section 'Economy and society' on pp. 261–4. Note how the operation of the market is said to enhance the wealth of nations.

<hr>

In this section of Chapter 22, David Coates argues that, within liberal thought, self-interested behaviour promotes the wealth of nations through the free and undisturbed play of market forces. Here the market is seen as an efficient coordinator of the activities of free individuals, an 'invisible hand' which helps to organize economic activities without state intervention. Although individuals are motivated only by the thought of their own gain, the overall outcome is advantageous to society as a whole. The result for a free market society is that a harmony of interests prevails between the individual and the larger society.

According to the liberal view, competitive markets provide the route to economic prosperity. But in addition to their economic role, markets are also seen as embodying a clear political implication in that a decentralized market process works independently of any political interference. There is a clear boundary line between the sphere of influence of the government and the sphere of economic operations as processed through markets. According to this view, a buoyant market economy enables ordinary citizens as workers and consumers to be independent of the power of the government, and to take economic decisions on their own behalf without interference from political authority. This view of competitive markets also stresses that economic power is dispersed amongst a large number of traders and customers. Thus, not only is political power kept out of economic transactions, but economic power is more widely dispersed within society.

This emphasis on the beneficial political implications of competitive markets can also be seen in liberalism's emphasis on the importance of 'freedom' from state interference in the lives of ordinary citizens. Being a free citizen implies a set of 'rights' which citizens have as workers and consumers; free to choose their own occupation, free to live and work where they wish, free to spend their own money as they please, and free to use and enjoy their own property and goods in the secure knowledge that they are protected by the laws of the country.

This emphasis on freedom has contributed powerfully to the appeal of economic liberalism. It can be seen clearly in the writings of liberals such as the economist Milton Friedman who has argued that without a free system of markets, individuals cannot enjoy freedom from totalitarian political rule.

=== READER ===

An extract from Milton Friedman's book *Capitalism and Freedom* is included in the Reader as Chapter 8. Now read this chapter and note the ways in which Friedman's argument in favour of markets is closely bound up with his argument for freedom.

Friedman argues here that 'the basic problem of social organization is how to coordinate the economic activities of large numbers of people'. Any society must practise some sort of division of labour, but a modern society has a very highly developed division of labour in which we are all dependent on the actions of millions of other people. For Friedman, the basic challenge is to 'reconcile this widespread interdependence with individual freedom', and Friedman can see only two opposing ways of doing this: either central political direction or voluntary cooperation. Friedman chooses voluntary cooperation and argues that this inevitably implies the free exchange of the market place. Note, however, that Friedman does not deny the importance of the restricted role that remains for government in a free society. Government is still essential for determining the 'rules of the game', that is, the legal framework of property rights, contracts, and law and order which are necessary for any civilized capitalist society to survive.

This liberal view of competitive markets has played a powerful role in shaping modern thinking on markets. But, as with any fertile tradition of thought, different versions of it have been developed over the years. In Section 3, I shall present two different approaches to market competition as two different liberal 'models' of the market. The liberal tradition itself, however, has provoked many criticisms that a system of competitive markets cannot deliver all the advantages that it is supposed to. Section 4 will examine some of these criticisms emanating from social reformism and its critique of liberalism's over-reliance on markets.

SUMMARY

- In economics the term 'markets' refers to the general process of buying and selling goods and services.

- The liberal tradition of thought emphasizes the economic and political benefits of free competitive markets.

3 TWO LIBERAL MODELS OF COMPETITIVE MARKETS

3.1 MODELS OF THE MARKET

As David Coates' essay on the liberal tradition shows, many influences went into the making of liberalism, and so it is not surprising that different variants of it have emerged in the course of time. In this section, I shall be presenting two different models of the competitive market which draw on different aspects of economic liberalism. The first model of the market is one that sees competition as a dynamic and fast-moving process that ushers in new epochs within capitalist history. It is thus a forward-looking model of competition as a social and economic process that is always on the move, hungrily searching out profitable new ventures. The second model focuses on the interactions of demand and supply, and the ways in which demand and supply are equalized in a competitive market. This model attaches greater significance to changes in market price, and the ways in which consumers and producers respond to these price changes.

In spite of their differences, both models show how the 'invisible hand' functions in free markets, securing outcomes that are efficient in achieving prosperity for consumers and producers. In each case markets provide the right incentives to motivate people to produce most efficiently the goods and services that contribute most to economic well being. In each case, too, this is achieved without political interference and without centralized direction of people's lives. For both these versions of a liberal account of the advantages of markets, it is the power of competition which produces these results. Market competition thus becomes a social force which operates independently of any political authority in securing economic prosperity.

This section will also provide an example of how 'models' are used in the social sciences, as it shows how models of the market provide an account of how the competitive process works in economic life. Such models help us to make sense of competition and how it works in the real world, but they cannot reflect all aspects of this process. In order to capture what is thought to be central to the competitive process, any model has to abstract from the complexity and particularities of actual situations. If the model is robust, it will then provide insights into actual processes, in spite of its more abstract nature. This is a general example of social science theorizing. It is as if we are having to work at two different levels at once: a concrete day to day level and a more abstract theoretical level, passing from the one to the other all the time. The discussion of models thus provides a further illustration of the course theme 'representation and reality', by showing how complex social and economic processes are represented in the form of simple models.

3.2 THE PROCESS OF 'CREATIVE DESTRUCTION'

The first model of the competitive market that I would like to look at is one that emphasizes that the economy is always on the move. Here the economy is seen as something restless and dynamic, never stopping still for a moment. In this view of the economy, competition is seen as a dynamic process in which firms are always trying to think ahead of their rivals and move into new areas faster than their competitors. Here the successful competitor is one that can see new market opportunities ahead of everyone else, and then has the drive and resources to act on this vision and reap the profits.

Given the central importance of staying ahead, this approach focuses especially on *innovations* in new products and new processes of production and marketing. Very often, new products and new processes go together as the new products also change existing working practices. In these cases, the effects of an innovation may be very wide ranging, spreading right across the economy and many aspects of social and family life.

As an example of such an innovation, consider the case of personal computers, a new product whose production was revolutionized during the 1970s and 80s with the development of microchip technology. Just a little while before, computers were bulky and expensive items, the preserve only of large institutions who could afford to buy and accommodate them. By the 1990s, personal computers were everywhere in the office and frequently at home too. The price of these computers had fallen dramatically in relation to household budgets. With further developments in the underlying technology, the new models were offering highly advanced and vastly enlarged computer capabilities in smaller and more portable models which brought the older versions tumbling down in price. In conjunction with these technological changes, marketing developments had helped to create a large and profitable market for home computers. Children were now growing up with personal computers both as toys and as a vital part of their formal education. It seemed that the age when computers were mysterious and inaccessible pieces of technical equipment was one that had existed long, long ago.

This story of the introduction of personal computers illustrates the view of competition as primarily a dynamic and transforming process. Classical economists such as Adam Smith and Karl Marx had recognized the importance of long-run dynamic aspects of capitalist competition, but in this century it was Joseph Schumpeter who stressed the ways in which firms are pressurized into searching out innovations, that is, new products and new processes of production. In describing this process, Schumpeter refers to it as an evolutionary process, emphasizing its constantly changing and adaptive nature. This was how he put it in a book first published in Britain in 1943:

> The essential point to grasp is that in dealing with capitalism we are dealing with an evolutionary process ... Capitalism, then, is by nature a form or method of economic change and not only never is but never can be stationary ... The fundamental impulse that sets and keeps the capitalist engine in motion comes from the new consumers' goods, the new methods of production or transportation, the new markets, the new forms of industrial organization that capitalist enterprise creates ... the history of the productive apparatus of a typical farm, from the beginnings of the rationalization of crop rotation, plowing and fattening to the mechanized thing of today — linking up with elevators and railroads — is a history of revolutions. So is the history of the productive apparatus of the iron and steel industry from the charcoal furnace to our own type of furnace, or the history of the apparatus of power production from the overshot water

wheel to the modern power plant, or the history of transportation from the mail-coach to the airplane. The opening up of new markets, foreign or domestic, and the organizational development from the craft shop and factory to such concerns as U.S. Steel illustrate the same process of industrial mutation—if I may use that biological term—that incessantly revolutionizes the economic structure *from within*, incessantly destroying the old one, incessantly creating a new one. This process of Creative Destruction is the essential fact about capitalism. It is what capitalism consists in and what every capitalist concern has got to live in.

(Schumpeter, 1976, pp.82–3, emphasis in original)

In this passage, Schumpeter outlines his view of the evolutionary nature of capitalism where firms are forced to innovate in order to stay in the race. Those firms which do not do this or which fall behind in the race to innovate, will go out of business. Schumpeter refers to this dynamic competitive process of 'innovate or go bust' as one of *creative destruction*. Many firms are destroyed in the competitive race, but the outcome for the economic system as a whole is a creative one, Schumpeter argues, as it is this that forces the pace of innovation that has improved living standards over the years.

This is a view of competitive markets as a dynamic process of continuous change. The key to this process is the introduction of innovations, new products and new processes which revolutionize the workplace and the types of work undertaken within them. As further examples we could cite the case of the motor car, which brought with it the assembly line method of production, and fast food which revolutionized the commercial kitchen.

These new products such as personal computers, cars and fast food, also transform the everyday lives of their consumers. Motor cars open up possibilities for leisure travel and for commuting to work. Extensive car ownership has also changed the environment, transforming urban areas and producing harmful ecological side effects. Personal computers have affected the organization of work and have increased the scope for the home office. They have also affected leisure activities. Fast food has helped to change people's eating habits, and the rituals of family eating have also changed along with it. Whereas at one time the sharing of the family meal was a centrepoint of family life, many families now rarely have such a formal meal and eat fast foods at home too. In all these various ways, competition between firms transforms the products on sale in the shops, the types of shops selling the products, and the ways people spend their time.

———————————— ACTIVITY I ————————————

Perhaps you would like to consider other examples of new products which have had far-reaching effects.

How about the domestic appliances which, some argue, have helped to release women from the drudgery of heavy household chores?

One of the points that Schumpeter emphasizes about competition is that it reduces costs and improves product quality. It is in these cost and product improvements that Schumpeter sees the progressive consequences of competitive activity. It is worth pausing for a moment to examine these cost reductions more closely. One crucial source of cost reduction that Schumpeter emphasizes is that arising from technological advances. This means that costs are reduced

The innovative force of competition, from the water wheel to nuclear energy, and from the letter mail to electronic mail

because advances in technological knowledge enable new production processes to be used that are cheaper than the old, sometimes creating entirely new products on the way. These cost reductions are often referred to as examples of *dynamic efficiency*. In the case of the motor car, the new technology of the internal combustion engine, combined with the new assembly line method of production, enabled the mass production of relatively cheap cars. In the case of computers, the development of the microchip was an essential ingredient in the technological changes that enabled computers to be both technically possible and relatively cheap to produce.

In addition, another source of cost reductions are *economies of scale* which relate to the scale of operations of the firm; in many cases, large firms produce most cheaply because they can spread the fixed costs or overhead costs over a larger scale of output. Alan Warde mentions economies of scale as a feature of mass production methods in the article 'The Future of Work' (Chapter 7 of the

Reader). Economies of scale depend on the presence of sizeable fixed costs. Fixed costs are the costs that remain constant whatever the level of output; these are usually the cost of buildings, land and equipment. If fixed costs are spread over a larger output, then the average cost per unit produced will fall. (The average cost or unit cost is calculated by dividing the total costs by the number of units of output produced.) For example, a doubling of output may not require a doubling of the factory size and a doubling of all machinery costs. In this case, the unit cost reductions arising from the large scale of operation by the firm are known as economies of scale, as the rate of output increases proportionately more than costs.

Perhaps here this point could be illustrated using a numerical example. For example, if an increase in output of 20 per cent required an increase in costs of 10 per cent, then the firm is operating under economies of scale as unit costs would fall with an increase in output.

—————————————— ACTIVITY 2 ——————————————

Just to check that you understand the idea of economies of scale, consider the case if output were to double and total costs were to increase threefold? Would you say that the firm here is operating under economies or diseconomies of scale?

In this case, there are diseconomies of scale; this is because total costs would increase proportionately faster than output, and this means that unit costs would rise with an increase in output.

To recap these points: we have seen that there are two possible sources of cost reductions that support Schumpeter's arguments about the efficiency of dynamic competition. There are cost reductions arising from new technological knowledge, and there are cost reductions arising from economies of scale. Although we can easily separate these two kinds of cost reductions at a conceptual level, in practice they are often combined as the new methods of production are feasible only if operated on a large scale. For example, the introduction of assembly line production was feasible only at certain high levels of production; similarly, microchip production also yields economies of large scale production.

One implication of this view of dynamic competition is that it is the large corporations and their managers that are significant for the competitive health of the economy. It is only the large corporations who have the financial resources to fund large research departments, set up the innovations and carry out the large-scale marketing and advertising necessary to sustain the large production runs. In this way, Schumpeter bases his model of competition on a market structure dominated by the large corporations. These corporations have been a feature of advanced economies for a long time, and they continue to grow in size. I wonder how many of the fifty largest industrial corporations in the world (in 1991) you know by name? Try jotting down the names that you know and then compare them with Table 1, which lists the fifty largest industrial groupings in the world based on data for 1990–1991 provided in the *Times 1000* listing.

Table 1   The world's top fifty industrial companies (1990–1991)

Rank	Company	Headquarters	Business	Sales £m	Year En
1	Itoh [C.] & Co. Ltd	Japan	*Sogo shosha* *	86,616,000	31/03/9
2	Mitsui & Co. Ltd	Japan	*Sogo shosha* *	84,702,000	31/03/9
3	Sumitomo Corporation	Japan	*Sogo shosha* *	81,392,000	31/03/9
4	Mitsubishi Corporation	Japan	*Sogo shosha* *	80,204,000	31/03/9
5	Marubeni Corporation	Japan	*Sogo shosha* *	79,546,000	31/03/9
6	General Motors Corpn	USA	Automobiles	65,911,000	31/12/9
7	Exxon Corporation	USA	Oil & gas industry	61,633,000	31/12/9
8	Royal Dutch/Shell Group	Netherlands/UK	Oil & gas industry	58,089,000	31/12/9
9	Nissho Iwai Corporation	Japan	*Sogo shosha* *	55,587,000	31/03/9
10	Ford Motor Co	USA	Automobiles	47,287,784	31/12/9
11	Toyota Motor Corpn	Japan	Automobiles	44,143,000	30/06/9
12	British Petroleum Company PLC (The)	UK	Oil & gas industry	41,267,000	31/12/9
13	International Business Machines Corpn	USA	Information technology	34,704,000	31/12/9
14	Mobil Corpn	USA	Oil & gas industry	33,866,000	31/12/9
15	American Telephone & Telegraph Co	USA	Telecommunications	33,792,000	31/12/9
16	Daimler-Benz AG	Germany	Automobiles	33,513,000	31/12/9
17	Hitachi Ltd	Japan	Electronics	31,457,000	31/03/9
18	Sears, Roebuck & Co.	USA	Mixed retail businesses	30,660,094	31/12/9
19	Tomen Corpn	Japan	*Sogo shosha* *	30,322,000	31/03/9
20	Morris [Philip] Co. Inc	USA	Food & tobacco	30,240,000	31/12/9
21	Volkswagen AG	Germany	Automobiles	26,919,000	31/12/9
22	Matsushita Electric Industrial Co. Ltd	Japan	Electronic consumer goods	26,831,000	31/03/9
23	Nichimen Corporation	Japan	*Sogo shosha* *	26,761,000	31/03/9
24	Fiat SpA	Italy	Automobiles	26,253,000	31/12/9
25	Nippon Telegraph & Telephone Corporation	Japan	Telecommunications	25,417,000	31/03/9
26	Siemens AG	Germany	Electrical engineering	25,045,758	30/09/9
27	Kanematsu Corporation	Japan	*Sogo shosha* *	24,781,000	31/03/9
28	Nissan Motor Co Ltd	Japan	Automobiles	24,252,000	31/03/9
29	Unilever Group	Netherlands/UK	Foods, detergents & personal products	23,886,000	31/12/9
30	General Electric Co (USA CO)	USA	Electricals & electronics	23,052,000	31/12/9
31	*ENI-Ente NazionaleIdrocarburi*	Italy	Oil & gas industry	22,960,000	31/12/9
32	Chevron Corpn	USA	Oil & gas industry	21,931,000	31/12/9
33	Veba AG	Germany	Electricity, oil, chemicals	20,989,500	31/12/9
34	Du Pont [E.I.] De Nemours & Co.	USA	Petroleum, fibres, industrial products	20,726,000	31/12/9
35	Elf Aquitaine *(Ste Nationale)*	France	Oil & gas industry	20,690,000	31/12/9
36	Texaco Inc	USA	Oil & gas industry	19,963,000	31/12/9
37	Nestlé SA	Switzerland	Food manufacture	19,955,000	31/12/9
38	K Mart Corpn	USA	Stores	19,115,000	29/01/9
39	Toshiba Corporation	Japan	Electronics	19,091,000	31/03/9
40	Tokyo Electric Power CoInc (The)	Japan	Public electricity supply	17,823,000	31/03/9
41	Philips Electronics NV	Netherlands	Electrical & electronic goods	17,808,000	31/12/9
42	*Electricité de France*	France	Public electricity supply	17,548,000	31/12/9
43	Honda Motor Co. Ltd	Japan	Automobiles	17,489,000	31/03/9
44	RWE AG	Germany	Public electricity supply	16,984,101	30/06/9
45	Proctor & Gamble Co. (The)	USA	Perfumes, cosmetics & toilet preparations	16,693,000	30/06/9
46	Hoechst AG	Germany	Chemicals	16,644,000	31/12/9
47	Renault *[Regie Nationale des Usines]* SA	France	Automobiles	16,615,000	31/12/9
48	Wal-Mart Stores Inc.	USA	Mixed retail businesses	16,582,700	31/01/9
49	BASF AG	Germany	Chemicals	16,446,627	31/12/9
50	Peugeot SA	France	Automobiles	16,245,000	31/12/9

* **Sogo shosha** refers to the large Japanese integrated trading operations, covering marketing, financing, transport and information services for their member companies.

Source: Times 1000, 1992–1993. Times Books, 1992.

To get an idea of the sizes involved here, note the annual sales for Itoh [C.] & Co. Ltd, the largest company, for the year ended March 1991: £86,616 million was approximately a fifth of the size of total output of the UK in that year. And Itoh was also more than five times as large as the organization listed fiftieth.

We have seen that, in Schumpeter's account, it is the large corporations that have the competitive edge in introducing innovations, deriving the benefits of dynamic efficiency and economies of scale. Schumpeter's high esteem for the innovatory role of large corporations sets him apart a little from some liberal arguments which tend to be suspicious that large corporations might abuse their position of market dominance. Schumpeter did not attach much weight to this suspicion. Even if a firm is dominant in a market at one particular point in time, he argued, it will be challenged by new innovations in the course of history. Again, we can see that Schumpeter's approach was to take a long-term view of the dynamic changes taking place in the course of time.

Schumpeter was worried about the growth of large corporations, however, but for a different reason. Schumpeter was concerned that the very large corporations would stunt the kind of individual initiative and resourcefulness that he thought was characteristic of the great individual entrepreneurs in history. Men like Henry Ford, Andrew Carnegie, and John D. Rockefeller were the entrepreneurial giants of business history whose grit and determination had been an essential ingredient in the development of early capitalism. Schumpeter was worried that the modern corporation would become too bureaucratic and would stifle the vision and talent of these entrepreneurial types. This points to what Schumpeter saw as a contradiction in the capitalist system itself, that as successful firms grew larger, they would become less innovative. For this reason, Schumpeter feared that the market's internal dynamic for producing innovation and growth would eventually slow down. Schumpeter was writing half a century ago, and did not live to see the burst of innovations and technological developments that have taken place during the second half of the twentieth century. Schumpeter's fears have so far proved unfounded, but the question of long-term trends and the future potential for never-ending growth is an issue that is still of concern.

SUMMARY

- Schumpeter's model of dynamic competition emphasizes innovations in both products and processes.

- In the process of competition over innovations, firms innovate or go bust; this is the process of 'creative destruction'.

- In this process of dynamic competition, costs are reduced by new technology and by economies of scale.

- Large firms are important in this evolutionary process because they have large funds for research and development (R & D) but Schumpeter feared that they might eventually blunt individual entrepreneurial initiative.

Schumpeter's model of competition as dynamic competition between corporate giants presents a picture of capitalist competition that seems quite 'realistic' to us. Remember, though, that it is a specific model of competitive behaviour. It concentrates on the longer term aspects of competition and it focuses on competition over products and processes in the new markets of the day. Schumpeter argues that dynamic competition and creative destruction are beneficial because innovations provide the most effective way of reducing costs and prices. Thus, Schumpeter is not only offering a model of what competition is and how it works. He is also offering an argument as to why competition (in his sense) is to be welcomed. Note here that Schumpeter's concept of competition is a very wide one and includes instances where firms may become very large and powerful.

3.3 COMPETITIVE MARKETS AND EQUILIBRIUM

In Schumpeter's model of dynamic competitive and creative destruction, we saw that the innovating firms were powerful organizations in the market. The other model of competition I wish to introduce is one which identifies competition with the absence of such corporate power in the market. According to this approach, the truly distinguishing feature of intense competition is that no one individual firm can have any influence over market outcomes. The neoclassical model of *perfect competition* (or competitive equilibrium as it is sometimes called), envisages a situation where there is such a large number of firms that each one is too small to have any discernible influence.

As individual firms have no influence in this model, a greater role is ascribed to 'the market' itself in securing certain competitive outcomes. Instead of focusing on the innovative activities of forward-looking corporations, this approach highlights the passive responses of atomistic firms to their external market environment. As individual firms simply respond to these external market conditions, it is the 'market' as such that seems to achieve certain results. Crucial to this way of thinking is the importance attached to price. In Schumpeter's model, innovations were the hallmark of healthy competitive activity; in this neoclassical model of perfect competition, movements of price register the extent to which a market is competitive. According to this model of competition, prices are determined impersonally in the market, and this ensures equality between the quantity demanded and the quantity supplied.

The neoclassical model of perfect competition examines the influences on the price of a commodity by grouping them into two broad categories—those influences on the side of supply and those on the side of demand. The *supply* side includes all those influences on the production of a commodity, such as the availability of the right kind of labour, raw materials, machinery, power, and also the technology in use at the time. The *demand* side includes all those influences which affect consumers' demand for a commodity, such as income, lifestyle, age, and the social conventions and expectations that can all be summed up as consumers' tastes. The activity below gives some illustrations.

─────────────────── ACTIVITY 3 ───────────────────

- As a result of an increase in food poisoning alleged to be related to the consumption of eggs, consumers wish to buy fewer eggs at any given price. In this case there has been a change on the *demand* side. The demand for eggs has fallen.
- Because of a world shortage of oil, less petrol is produced at any given price. In this case there has been a change on the *supply* side; the supply of petrol has fallen.

Now try some exercises for yourself: would the following changes affect the demand or supply side of the market?

1   Manufacturers develop a more economical process for making washing machines.

2   Producers introduce an extensive advertising campaign for a new kind of fruit juice.

In the first example, if manufacturers develop a more economical process for making washing machines, there would be a change on the supply side of the market. In the second example, if an extensive advertising programme is introduced by the producers this will be aimed at making the product more attractive to consumers. If the advertising campaign is successful, demand for the juice will increase. In this way, all the influences on price can be grouped either on the side of demand or on the side of supply.

But what is the relation between demand, supply and price? One way of understanding this is to see the competitive market as a *balancing mechanism* that balances demand and supply. In this mechanism, changes in price result in a balance—or equilibrium—between demand and supply. If demand is less than supply, then the new price must be lower than the original one in order for demand and supply to balance again; if demand is greater than supply, then the new price must be higher than the original price to restore balance. These results are summarized in Table 2.

Table 2   The balancing of demand and supply

- If D is less than S, then P would have to fall for D and S to be in equilibrium.
- If D is more than S, then P would have to increase for D and S to be in equilibrium.

——————————— ACTIVITY 4 ———————————

The results in Table 2 may have a certain plausibility, but do you feel you can explain them in your own words?

My own explanation would be along the following lines. In the first example, if demand is less than supply at the original price, this means that there are unsold supplies on the market. If these unsold supplies are to find a buyer, then the price would have to be lower. At a lower price, more would be demanded both because consumers could afford to buy more and because, compared with other goods whose price has not fallen, this good is now a better buy. Similarly, at a lower price, less would be supplied because it is now less financially attractive for firms to produce the good if their objective is to make as much profit as possible. The combined effect of the increase in quantity demanded and the fall in the quantity supplied, would ensure that demand and supply are brought to equilibrium at a lower price.

In the second example, if demand is greater than supply at the original price, this means that there are consumers in the market who would like to make purchases at the going price, but who are unable to do so. If demand and supply are to be in equilibrium again, there would have to be an increase in the price which would reduce demand and increase supply.

This neoclassical model of perfect competition has been enormously important for economics. This may be seen by reading the following extract from Professor Kenneth Arrow's Nobel Prize Lecture delivered in 1972. Arrow's work has contributed to a mathematical exploration of the neoclassical model, and he also looks back to Adam Smith for an early statement of the importance of the notion of a balance or equilibrium between demand and supply:

> From the time of Adam Smith's *Wealth of Nations* in 1776, one recurrent theme of economic analysis has been the remarkable degree of coherence among the vast numbers of individual and seemingly separate decisions about the buying and selling of commodities. In everyday, normal experience, there is something of a balance between the amounts of goods and services that some individuals want to buy

and the amounts that other, different individuals want to sell. Would-be buyers ordinarily count correctly on being able to carry out their intentions, and would-be sellers do not ordinarily find themselves producing great amounts of goods that they cannot sell. This experience of balance is indeed so widespread that it raises no intellectual disquiet among laymen; they take it so much for granted that they are not disposed to understand the mechanism by which it occurs.

(Arrow, 1974, p.253)

In this passage, Arrow refers to the 'balance' between the amounts that people wish to buy and sell. In other words, Arrow is describing the balance between demand and supply. As he says, there is a 'remarkable degree of coherence' among producers' and consumers' decisions, and this coherence is achieved by the operation of the price 'mechanism'. This is the same idea as Friedman's argument about the need for 'coordination' in an economy characterized by an extensive division of labour. When demand and supply are in balance, then all economic activities are fully coordinated throughout the economy.

As a way of exploring the demand and supply model, we could continue with our image of the price system as a *balancing* mechanism, where the equality of demand and supply is represented as a balancing of demand and supply. One way of doing this is to represent an individual market as a 'balance' or as a pair of weighing scales, scales that have been replaced in our shops now by electronic weighing machines. In Figure 1 there is a diagram of such a pair of scales, and here the pans represent demand and supply.

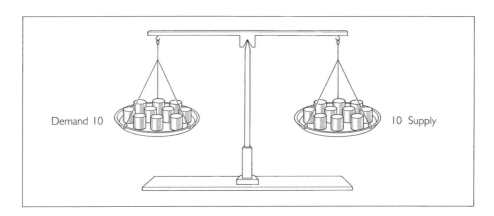

Figure 1 A representation of the competitive market as the balancing of demand and supply

In Figure 1, the demand and supply pans are in balance, or in equilibrium. In this case, demand and supply are equal and everything is at rest; the market price is said to be the *equilibrium price*.

In Figure 2, the demand pan is lighter than the supply pan. In this case, less of the good is demanded (that is, demand has become lighter) whilst supply has remained unchanged (and so has become relatively heavier). Consumers have switched their expenditure away from this good. This would be the case with the example of food poisoning allegedly associated with eggs that we saw earlier on.

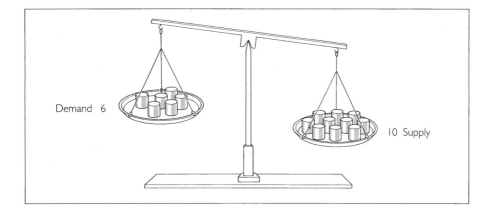

Figure 2 A fall in demand relative to supply at the existing market price

In the case shown in Figure 2, demand is lighter than supply, so that to make them balance again we have to increase demand relative to supply. One way of achieving this is to reduce the price of the good. This reduction in price would have two effects. It would increase the quantity demanded, as the lower price would both encourage and enable more people to consume more of the good. In addition, it would reduce the quantity supplied, as the good would become less profitable for suppliers to produce. The new equilibrium price would be such that the net effect of the increased demand and the reduced supply is that demand and supply once again balance. This is shown in Figure 3. At a lower equilibrium price, demand and supply are again in balance.

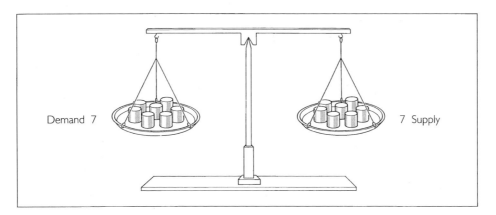

Figure 3   Restoration of equilibrium at a reduced market price following an initial reduction in demand

In Figure 3, demand and supply are again in balance, at the lower price, but note that the actual quantities demanded and supplied are smaller than in the original equilibrium position.

─────────────── ACTIVITY 5 ───────────────

What do you think would happen in the opposite case where supply fell for some reason? Do you think that the final equilibrium price would be higher or lower than the original equilibrium price?

If supply were less than, that is lighter than, demand, then an increase in the price would be needed to increase the quantity supplied and decrease the quantity demanded. A higher price would make the good more profitable for firms to produce. The higher price would also mean that consumers would be discouraged from buying the good, and that it would now compare less favourably with other goods available for sale on the market. If supply were to increase and demand fall, this means that the supply pan would become heavier and the demand pan would become lighter until the two pans are in balance again. In other words, if the price increases the quantity supplied would increase and the quantity demanded would fall until they are once again in balance at the new higher equilibrium price.

In Activity 3, you may remember, we looked at the way that events can affect demand and supply, but we did not follow this through to see how these changes in demand and supply would affect the equilibrium price. The first example in Activity 3 was the eggs case. If the demand for eggs falls, there would have to be a fall in the equilibrium price of eggs for demand and supply to be in balance again. In the second case, if there is a world shortage of oil, this means that supply has fallen at any given price, and so the equilibrium price would have to rise for supply to balance demand. (This is what happened when OPEC restricted output and raised the price of oil in 1974 and 1979.) The third case involved a cheapening of the production of washing machines; here the increase in supply means that the equilibrium price would have to fall for demand to equal supply. In the final example, consumer demand for juice increases as a result of the advertising campaign. Here the equilibrium price would have to rise.

We have seen in this section how changes in the equilibrium price can secure a balance between demand and supply. In this way, price changes provide incentives to both consumers and suppliers, whose independent reactions then result in a new balancing of the market where there are no unsatisfied customers and no frustrated sellers. Consumers economize on goods that become more expensive, and suppliers will have an incentive to produce more of those goods whose price rises. In this way, the price mechanism works by balancing demand and supply without any central direction, relying only on individual consumers and suppliers acting in their own interests. As a model of the decentralized coordination of many independent consumers and suppliers, this model of the competitive market has gained many admirers and has stimulated an enormous amount of mathematical refinement from economists such as Kenneth Arrow.

What is the link between competition and efficiency in the neoclassical model of competition? Perfectly competitive firms cannot influence the market price which is determined by market forces. This means that if a firm wants to make profits, it must reduce its costs as much as possible. But all firms are doing this, and so costs for the entire market are pushed down to the minimum level. When costs are at the minimum possible level given the existing technology of the day, we say that firms are *productively efficient*.

Competition between firms also means that the price is pushed down to the minimum level that is consistent with the continued survival of the firms in the market. This means that firms cannot continue to earn excessive profits. If costs of production fall, say because the cost of raw materials has fallen, this cost reduction will be passed on to the consumer in the form of a reduction in price. Why do you think this will happen? Why don't existing firms try to hang on to their extra profits by charging a higher price?

--- ACTIVITY 6 ---

It is worth spending some time thinking about this question as it highlights the process of competition between perfectly competitive firms.

Consider a situation where, at the original equilibrium price, profits increase because the cost of raw materials has fallen. (Or you could consider the case where profits have increased because demand has increased.)

What do you think are likely to be the longer-term consequences if other firms are free to enter the market, attracted by the higher profits? If you are not sure about this, you could look back at Activities 3–5 and consider the effects of an increase in supply.

I wonder what you made of this question. There is a clue in the last sentence where I suggested you might think about an increase in supply.

At the original equilibrium price, profits have increased and so new firms enter the market in pursuit of higher profit. This means that supply increases, and this implies a reduction in the equilibrium price. As long as the price is high enough for exceptional profits to persist, then new entrants into the market may be expected. But once the equilibrium price has been reduced to the level where only the going rate of profit can be made, then the flow of new firms entering the market will cease. With this new equilibrium price, there is a larger output than before and firms once again earn the going, or normal, rate of profit. This means not only that prices are pushed down to the minimum, but that firms cannot earn excessive profits in the long run because high profits are always competed away by new firms entering the market.

SUMMARY

- In the neoclassical model of perfect competition, equilibrium is achieved when demand and supply are equal.
- If demand is greater than supply, then price has to rise for demand and supply to be equal; if demand is less than supply, then price has to fall for demand and supply to be equal.
- In the neoclassical model of perfect competition, costs are reduced to the minimum, given existing technology: that is, firms are productively efficient.
- Prices are at the minimum level that is consistent with the continued survival of firms in the market, and firms earn only the going, or normal, rate of profit because high profits are competed away by new firms entering the industry.

In this section, I have outlined the basic neoclassical model of competitive demand and supply, and we have seen how changes in the equilibrium price can balance demand and supply. If demand is greater than supply, then the equilibrium price will have to increase in order for balance to be restored; if supply is greater than demand, then the equilibrium price will have to fall. In this way, price changes can restore equilibrium to the market in an apparently natural or impersonal manner, as no one individual consumer or trader has any influence in the market.

Comparing this model with Schumpeter's model of dynamic competition, we can see that they are very different. The neoclassical model focuses on the responses of firms who are very small relative to the market they are supplying. Such firms have to accept the market price as given to them. Here the price is determined by the anonymous force of 'the market', and excessive profits are always competed away in the long run. In Schumpeter's model of dynamic competition, firms can set their own prices, and will do so within a framework of intense competition over new products and processes. As large firms have survival advantages in the process of creative destruction, this dynamic competition favours large firms. Here there are enormous profits to be made as the reward for entrepreneurship and innovation. In terms of a much longer time horizon, however, even large firms are subject to competition from new products and new processes, so that even here, profits are not secure forever but must be earned by a never-ending process of innovation.

———————————————— ACTIVITY 7 ————————————————

To help you compare these two models of market competition, try to list the key points of the theories by filling in the blanks in the following chart.

	Schumpeter's model of dynamic competition	neoclassical model of perfect competition
model of competition	dynamic competition, that is, forward-looking competition over innovations in products and processes; the process of creative destruction	perfect competition; at the equilibrium price, demand and supply are equal; firms have no influence over price which is set by market forces
type of efficiency		
organizational structure		

A completed version of this chart appears at the end of the unit.

3.4 COMPETITIVE MARKETS AND EFFICIENCY

The previous sections have examined two different models of competition, Schumpeter's dynamic model of competition and the neoclassical model of perfect competition. These models agree that competition has beneficial effects in that costs and prices are reduced to the minimum level, but they come to different conclusions as to how those beneficial effects are produced. As a way of summarizing and illustrating these different views of competition, I shall look at European competition and the completion of the single European market at the end of 1992.

By eliminating forms of regulation concerning product specifications that operated as barriers to trade, it was intended to produce a large single European market. The area had been fractured into small uneconomic subsections as a result of individual countries' national legislation which had produced different regulations operating in different countries. By abolishing these country-specific regulations, it was hoped to create a large internal market of about 320 million people, almost as large as that of the USA and Japan combined. The intention was that such a large internal market would stimulate competition over a wide area, improving economic efficiency and reducing costs.

As we have seen in previous sections, however, there are different ways of reducing costs and improving efficiency, and these may well have different implications for competition. The first point here is that the increased size of the market might well facilitate economies of scale and that this would help to reduce unit costs. (If you are not sure about this, you might like to review Activity 2.) This would help to make European firms more competitive in the world market, as they would have access to the same sort of economies of scale as US and Japanese firms. On the other hand, the potential for economies of scale varies across products, and some economists have argued that many European industries were already operating at pretty close to the efficient scale by 1992.

The second point is that competition across member states may well lead to a heightened form of Schumpeterian or dynamic competition. In other words, the increased competition may lead to new product and process innovations and increased technological change. Schumpeter's model of competition is based on the idea of creative destruction where firms have to innovate or perish. Here it is only by keeping up with, or ahead of, the new products and processes of the day, that any firm can hope to maintain its share in the market, let alone expand its operations and increase its market share of sales. In this case, industries might regroup themselves with possible takeovers and mergers ensuing as firms try to consolidate their own position in the market.

The third source of efficiency that I would expect derives from 'productive efficiency' which we looked at in connection with the neoclassical model of competition. Productive efficiency refers to the reduction of unit costs to the minimum, given the existing technology. Although individual firms cannot influence the market price, the forces of competition tend to push both price and costs down to the lowest possible level.

Although the Schumpeterian and neoclassical models give different accounts of the benefits of increased competition, we could easily imagine that the resulting outcome will be some combination of the effects predicted by the two models, with improvements in economies of scale, dynamic efficiency and productive efficiency. In this way, both innovation and price competition might well emerge in the single European market.

One way of understanding these three different sources of increased efficiency is to consider the effects of increased competition on a firm's *average costs*.

Average costs are equivalent to a firm's total costs divided by the quantity of output. Increased efficiency results in a reduction in average costs. This can be illustrated using a diagram such as the one in Figure 4.

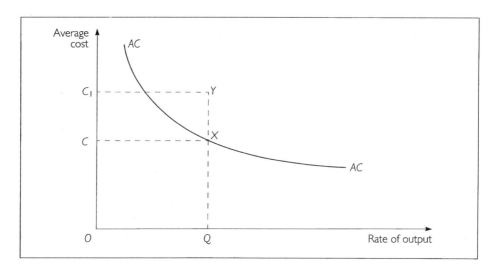

Figure 4 Average costs

Figure 4 shows an average cost curve, labelled AC. (This diagram is also discussed on Audio-cassette 3 for you to work through at your own pace.) This curve shows the minimum possible average cost of producing any level of output over some specified period of time, say a year, such that any inputs to the production process may be changed. Average cost (that is, total cost divided by the rate of output) is shown on the vertical axis, and the rate of output is shown on the horizontal axis. Notice that points above the line represent costs that are higher than necessary, while points below the line represent costs that are not possible to achieve given current technological knowledge. The points shown by the AC line are therefore the lowest possible costs given current technology; in other words, all such points on the line show productive efficiency. This means that a point such as X shows that the minimum average cost is C when the rate of output is Q. In this case the firm would be productively efficient.

Now consider what a point such as Y would denote. Think about this for a moment before reading on.

A point such as Y is above the AC line, showing that the cost of producing an amount Q is C_1. This would be an inefficient way of producing this quantity as it could be produced more cheaply at a level of average cost anywhere between C and C_1. The cheapest, and therefore most efficient, way of producing the good is at point C. In the presence of perfect competition, point Y is not a viable option for a firm as other more efficient firms producing the same product could undercut and sell more cheaply by producing at a lower average cost.

Now consider Figure 5 where a second average cost line, AC^*, has been added beneath AC.

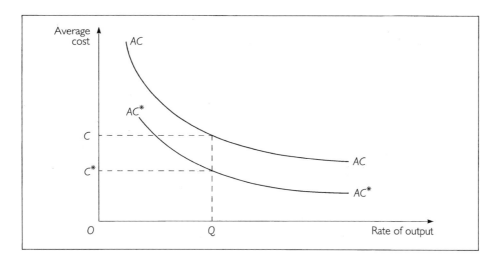

Figure 5 Average costs and technological development

In Figure 5 the new *AC* line, *AC**, denotes the reduced costs resulting from an advance in technological knowledge. Now we can see that an output of *Q* can be produced more cheaply than before, at an average cost of *C** which is below *C*. On this new line, *AC**, all points are productively efficient as well as efficient in a dynamic sense. The process of innovation in Schumpeter's model results in pushing down the AC curve in this way, enabling firms to produce the same (or improved) output at lower cost.

Just one more point that is worth noticing about these *AC* lines which are drawn sloping downwards from left to right. This shape illustrates economies of large-scale production where average costs are lower at higher rates of output.

———————————————— ACTIVITY 8 ————————————————

As an exercise to check this out, you could try marking out a number of points such as *X* on the *AC* line. For each point, mark out with a dotted line the level of cost that would apply at that level of output, just as I did with point *X*. Then see how the average cost is different for different levels of output. You should find that the average cost is lower for higher rates of output.

Figures 4 and 5 show very clearly our three different sources of cost reductions — productive efficiency, dynamic efficiency and economies of scale. But they also raise a question as to the kind of competition that would best promote efficiency in the longer run: Is 'competitive efficiency' best promoted by a relatively small number of large corporations investing heavily in research, or is it best promoted by an industry composed of many small firms? This question was addressed by a study conducted by the European Commission which attempted to examine the consequences for efficiency of completing the internal market, and this was what it concluded:

> European integration would thus assist the emergence of a virtuous
> circle of innovation and competition — competition stimulating
> innovation which in turn would increase competition. This is not to say
> that the desired form of competition corresponds to the theoretical and
> simplified model of perfect competition. The relationship between
> competition and innovation is not linear and indeed there exists an

optimal level of competition beyond which competition has an adverse effect on innovation because of the difficulty of allocating gains and the greater risks which obtain in highly competitive markets. The optimum market structure from the standpoint of innovation ought rather to promote strategic rivalry between a limited number of firms.

(*European Economy*, 1988, p.129)

In this conclusion the authors argue that the desired form of competition in their view would not be that of perfect competition, but one of rivalry between a limited number of firms in order to stimulate innovation. To me this sounds similar to the Schumpeterian view of the benefits of competition.

Euro-oil and the Euro-car? Will European products become more standardized or more heterogeneous during the 1990s?

In practice, we would expect improvements in efficiency to come from all sources, from productive efficiency, dynamic efficiency and economies of scale. The particular mix will depend on the particular products that European firms come to specialize in, and movements in consumer tastes. The garment industry, for example, has a much smaller scope for economies of scale than the motor vehicle industry. To a certain extent, high levels of trade within Europe means that most economies of scale had already been realized by 1992. Further, some economists have argued that Europe remains a culturally differentiated area, showing well-developed tastes for a range of differentiated products, and that this means that overall demand will remain heterogeneous. In this case, economists would be sceptical about the gains that are possible from economies of scale as this implies a high level of standardization; the scope for mass production of standardized 'Euro-goods' — such as the 'Euro-car' and the 'Euro-sausage' — depends crucially on the extent of the 'Euro-consumer' with uniform tastes. As the evidence at the moment is that tastes become more — not less — differentiated as income rises, it is thought unlikely that the mass production of 'Euro-goods' will become a reality (Kay, 1989).

Time will tell as to the actual economic benefits arising from the completion of the single European market, and this is something that you can watch out for as you study this course.

SUMMARY

- Schumpeter's model of dynamic competition and the neoclassical model of perfect competition give different insights into how competitive outcomes may emerge as a result of Europe 1992.

- In either case, much will depend in practice on movements in consumer tastes.

This section has considered two liberal models of the market. Their main point of similarity lies in their espousal of the benefits of free untrammelled markets where individuals can pursue their own interest in their own way. Unfettered by government restrictions or by wider considerations of what might or might not constitute the 'public good', individual economic behaviour nonetheless leads to outcomes that are beneficial for society as a whole. In this way the market functions as an 'invisible hand', guiding economic actions in such a way that the final outcome, though unplanned by anyone, is advantageous to society as a whole. This is the liberal theory of 'unintended consequences': as individuals are planning only in terms of their own self-interest, the overall outcome is unintended, but yet it is still beneficial.

The differences between these two models lies in the detail of their view of how the market works in this beneficial way. The Schumpeterian approach emphasizes the dynamic long-term process of competition which revolutionizes the processes of production and the products produced. The emphasis here is on creative destruction and innovation as the mainsprings of the competitive process. The neoclassical model focuses on the mechanics of demand and supply rather than the grand sweep of capitalist transformation. Here price changes are seen as fundamental to the process of matching demand and supply, that is, the process of matching consumer preferences with firms' output. Prices act to coordinate the myriad number of decisions that are taken daily in the economy, and it is this act of 'impersonal' market coordination that obviates any need for political interference in the exercise of economic choice by free economic agents.

4 SOCIAL REFORMIST CRITIQUES OF THE MARKET

4.1 SOCIAL REFORMISM

Critiques of the market are as old as the market itself. During the Middle Ages in Europe, these critiques tended to focus on the moral failings of market behaviour from the point of view of the requirements of Christian theology. Even Adam Smith could be deeply scathing about the self-interest of the marketplace and the vanity of personal ambition, although he recognized their economic importance. As you learnt in Unit 5, the social reformist tradition of thought has more recently functioned as a general forum within which modern critiques of liberalism, self-interest and *laissez-faire* could find a home. Social reformism does not form an integrated theoretical position as liberalism does. In part, it comprises a number of different critiques or qualifications of liberalism and unfettered market capitalism.

Social reformist critiques tend to challenge the argument that competitive markets are efficient by pointing to markets that produce inefficient outcomes. The social reformists attach greater weight to those instances where competitive markets are not so efficient in guiding society's production and consumption decisions. One example of this is unemployment. The social reformist tradition argues that it is inefficient to have widespread unemployment because that involves a waste of both human resources and physical resources.

It is often the case that social reformist arguments also rely on a moral dimension. For example, they argue that market outcomes are inequitable and that this is indefensible from a social point of view. This is different from the medieval notion that individual moral behaviour is not compatible with profit-seeking activity. Rather it derives from social reformism's greater commitment to social as opposed to individual perspectives on economic issues. From a social point of view, they argue, unemployment is wrong because it causes individual hardship and produces social tensions. This feeling that society should not tolerate mass unemployment nor extremes of poverty is thus a hallmark of the social reformist's view of social justice.

Thus social reformist arguments are generally prepared to judge market outcomes against standards of fairness or justice. Sometimes these fairness arguments may reinforce the efficiency arguments, but sometimes they pull in the opposite direction, and this then produces difficulties for social reformism. For example, policies to reduce income inequalities may conflict with policies to make labour markets more sensitive to skill requirements and personal incentives; whereas the former may result in narrowing the wage differentials between different groups of workers, the latter may require increasing them. This commitment to 'social justice' is in sharp contrast with liberal arguments which emphasize that arguments about justice are not relevant to the outcomes of market events. According to the liberal view, market outcomes stand apart from questions of justice and injustice. This is because the liberal tradition tends to see justice in terms of intentional human conduct, rather than in terms of overall social outcomes which cannot be attributed to the intentions of individuals. (Note that liberals as well as social reformists generally support at least some social welfare measures outside the market system, although liberals tend to rely much less on these and more on market incentives.)

Here we can see an instance of the influence of values in social science explanations, as explained earlier in Unit 5. Liberalism and social reformism have different kinds of social values, and these different social values are deeply interlinked with their different analyses of economic situations. Liberalism tends to analyse economic situations on the basis of individual self interest, whereas social reformism tends to examine situations in terms of broader societal factors. This difference is reflected in their approach to issues of morality and justice; liberalism tends to see justice as an issue only of individual conduct, whereas social reformism also understands justice as having an important social dimension.

In this section I shall look at three kinds of social reformist critiques of the liberal view of market. In these critiques, we shall see that issues of efficiency and fairness are often interwoven. The first critique highlights cases of 'market failure', the second relates to issues of inequality, and the third concerns the problem of unemployment.

4.2 MARKET FAILURES

Market failures refer to all those situations where markets function badly, and so it is a kind of general catch-all term. Here I would like to concentrate on just one aspect of this, and look at some cases where markets systematically fail to produce efficient results. You will see that the emphasis is on efficiency rather than fairness, but even here, it is hard to keep out questions of fairness altogether.

In Section 3.3 we looked at the relation between demand and supply, and the ways in which equilibrium could be restored in a market by changes in the equilibrium price. In the various examples that we looked at, the focus was always on the decisions of the individual consumer and the individual firm or producer. As you know, this corresponds with the liberal emphasis on the significance of the individual, or the individual household or individual firm, as the decision-making unit. Market situations tend to work very well where this individual approach accurately describes the situation. My decision to buy another bag of tomatoes, for example, is not likely to affect others beyond the implications of the economic transactions involved. The tomato growers are affected, and so are all those who are connected even indirectly with the tomato industry, but they are affected as a result of those market transactions. Beyond these market implications, no one else is likely to be very much affected.

Similarly, your decision to buy a new motor car will affect motor vehicle workers and those involved in the motor components industry, together with all those other service and support industries whose fortunes are tied to the motor vehicle industry, but it will not affect anyone else much. Or will it?

ACTIVITY 9

Consider this for a moment.

To what extent will the decision by you or your household to buy a new motor car affect others beyond all the economic implications of the sale transaction itself? That is, to what extent will your decision affect anyone other than those involved in the motor vehicle industry and all the industries that are connected with the motor vehicle industry?

The purchase of another motor car will affect people not party to the economic implications of the sale itself. As in the tomato case, workers in related industries are affected, and so too are their supplying industries. But in addition here, others are considerably affected even though they have no economic connection with the production or sale of motor vehicles. Cars cause traffic congestion, noise and pollution. This means that many people are affected by the use of the motor car, whether or not they themselves travel by car. Further, and this is important, they are affected in ways that cannot be captured through the workings of the market. The sufferer of pollution, for example, is not compensated by the car driver. The terms of the sale transaction do not make the car user contribute to the cost of degrading the environment because the purchase price reflects only the direct costs of making the car. It excludes the indirect costs on society of using that car and causing pollution. Similarly, even though affected adversely by the pollution caused by others, I as an individual cannot pay for a cleaner environment. I cannot buy clean air for myself; I cannot pay for an unpolluted city to live in, no matter how rich I am.

These effects are sometimes known as *externalities* because they are external to the market; although produced by market transactions, they remain outside the market and so cannot be resolved by the market. Sometimes too they are called *spillover effects* (because they spill over from each individual exchange transaction and affect others who are outside that transaction) or *neighbourhood effects* as in Friedman's extract (because they affect third parties). Pollution is a classic instance of market failure. Markets work less efficiently in the presence of externalities, because the prices paid do not fully reflect all the costs or benefits to society as a result of the transaction. If the price of cars were to reflect the full cost to society, they would have to be higher in order to compensate for the costs of pollution. This could take the form of a 'pollution tax'. This tax would be collected by the government and could be used towards cleaning up the pollution caused. Or it could be used to set up extra hospitals which specialize in treating illnesses such as asthma which are thought to be exacerbated by car pollution. The 'pollution tax' would also make cars more expensive and this higher price would help to choke off some of the demand for them. This too would help to limit the pollution consequences of car ownership.

This argument concerning market failure is concerned with establishing how efficiently a market is working, and whether the prices charged are set at the 'right' level. It is therefore an argument relating to efficiency. But note even here how equity issues also intrude. Although no one can buy clean air in a busy polluted city, people's access to a healthy and pleasant environment depends on their income level. Normally, the most polluted areas of the city provide low value housing for people on low incomes, while the cleaner areas and leafy suburbs provide homes for more prosperous people. Further, although taxing pollutants may help to get prices more in line with social costs, the increased price is a relatively greater burden for those on low incomes. Taxing non-renewable sources of energy, for example, has been proposed as a 'green' tax on efficiency grounds, but such a tax has regressive implications for the distribution of income because those on lower incomes have to pay out a higher proportion of their income. A tax on domestic fuel, for example, represents a greater proportionate tax for those on lower incomes and for those who are elderly who require greater warmth (and who also tend to be on lower incomes).

There are many instances of market failure, and critics of the market are not slow to point them out. Externalities arise in situations of mutual interdependence where the liberal assumption of individualism is inappropriate. To the extent that the economic world is becoming more interdependent, externalities are on the increase rather than decreasing.

—————————————— ACTIVITY 10 ——————————————

Can you think of any other examples of externalities?

Some externalities that occur to me are: the pleasure that I derive from seeing a neighbour's well-tended garden, the effect of television sex and violence on young people's attitudes and behaviour, the health effects on others of smoking cigarettes, the effect on others' health if contagious diseases do not receive proper treatment, the effect on industry of an efficient school system, the effect on the environment of industrial pollution, and the effect on a local economy of providing a modern transport system. As you can see, the list of externalities could be a very long one and would include items of varying importance. Sometimes they may be positive, as in the case of the effect on industry of an efficient school system, and sometimes they are negative, as in the case of the environmental effects of industrial pollution. Some are of greater significance than others but it is very hard to know how to measure these differences: the increase in asthma from increased traffic congestion may be more significant than the pleasure given by a neighbouring garden, but how do we measure the overall health consequences of increased pollution?

The presence of externalities has provided one set of potential reasons for state involvement in the economy including environmental policies, health programmes, educational provision, public transport, industrial support, and the regulations concerning standards and safety that are taken for granted until something goes wrong. These are the kinds of policies favoured by social reformists who look to the government to provide social responses to what are perceived as social rather than individual problems.

A relatively new issue that has been causing increased concern is that of the 'greenhouse effect' where the earth's temperature is thought to be increasing as a result of the emission of carbon dioxide, chlorofluorocarbons (CFCs), methane and nitrous oxide into the atmosphere. Scientific estimates differ, but it has been argued that the increase of greenhouse gas concentrations from their pre-industrial revolution levels will involve an increase in average world temperatures. One implication of this global warming is that the earth's oceans are warming and the ice caps melting, with consequential risks of flooding in low-lying coastal areas. In addition, the regional climatic effects of such a warming are likely to be extensive although they are difficult to predict. The evidence on global warming has raised again, in a particularly acute form, the question of the extent to which free market solutions can be found for environmental problems.

SUMMARY

- Externalities occur where there is a discrepancy between the price charged for a good and the social costs or social benefits involved in the production and consumption of the good.

- In the presence of externalities, competitive market solutions are not efficient and 'wrong' amounts of the good are consumed.

- Social reformists are more likely to call for government action of some sort in the presence of externalities

---

4.3 MARKETS AND INEQUALITY

A prime concern of the social reformist critique is that markets cannot eradicate inequality and poverty. It argues that liberalism's emphasis on individualism overlooks the important ways in which individuals are manifestly unequal in a system of markets. Here the social reformist concern with issues of fairness finds its fullest outlet.

Concern has been expressed about those cases where there is a conflict of interest in the market transaction, where it is argued that the distribution of the benefits from the market transactions will reflect the power of the transacting parties. Here we have a model of the competitive market as a 'power balance'. This view has been expressed by Professor Amartya Sen whose work on poverty and famines has helped to make economists more aware of the issues of inequality. Remember you also met Sen's work in Unit 2 where you studied the causes of hunger. In the quotation below, Sen is arguing that the market works well enough where individual interests are 'congruent' or harmonious, but that they do not work well where interests are in conflict:

> The market mechanism, with each person pursuing his self-interest, is geared to making sure that the congruent interests are exploited, but it does not offer a mechanism for harmonious or fair resolution of the problem of conflict that is inoperably embedded in the congruent exercise. The 'presumed harmony' ... stands for, at best, a half-truth. The market division of benefits tends to reflect, roughly speaking, the economic 'power balance' of different individuals and groups...
>
> *(Sen, 1989, p.111)*

Here Sen is turning the idea of market balance or equilibrium on its head. He is arguing that markets inevitably reflect the unequal balance of power in society. According to this view, the balancing of demand and supply hides the real inequalities and unequal powers in market-dominated societies. Sen's arguments highlight the unequal distribution of income and wealth in market society, and regional and national differences in economic welfare.

This approach to the market uses a different concept of 'freedom' from that employed by Milton Friedman and other writers in the liberal tradition such as F. A. Hayek. As you saw in Chapter 22 of the Reader, the liberal concept of freedom has been described as *negative freedom* because it is seen as a freedom *from* interference. The concept of freedom appropriate to an approach such as Sen's, would be a concept of freedom as enabling powers or capabilities. As this concept of freedom emphasizes the actual opportunities available for people to act, it is sometimes referred to as *positive freedom*.

As an example of the difference between positive and negative freedom, consider a person's freedom to take an Open University course. Everyone is free to take such a course, free in the negative sense that the state does not directly intervene to prevent people from taking the course. But the actual conditions attaching to the successful completion of such a course mean that some students do have greater access to these courses and are better placed to complete them successfully. Conditions such as the payment of a fee, a quiet place to study undisturbed, and the support of family and friends through the trials of part-time study are all factors which will affect a person's ability to attempt a course of intensive study, and so they can all be seen as factors affecting a person's positive freedom to study. Here, the attitudes of employers towards study leave and state policy on the charging of student fees will also have a significant effect on people's freedom to undertake courses of study. It is because the concept of negative freedom seemed too narrow to reflect people's ability actually to exercise their notional freedoms, that the concept of positive freedom was developed. It tends to focus on the extent to which people are able in a material or practical sense to exercise the rights included under negative freedom. It thus attaches considerable importance to the distribution of material and economic life-chances, as it sees these as important in determining a person's ability to make choices.

The approach represented by Sen's writings raises some large questions about the distribution of the benefits arising from competitive markets and technological advances. As you saw in Unit 2, Sen has been involved in examining the occurrence of famines and he has argued against the Food Availability Decline (FAD) approach by stressing that these famines were not always the result of absolute food shortages. Instead Sen has argued that the famines were the result of the inadequate command or 'entitlement' that individuals were able to exercise over the marketed food output in their country. Even in the richer market-based economies of the West, he argues, it is recognized that individuals cannot be left to survive on market entitlements only. In all these Western countries, social security payments cushion the less fortunate from the vagaries and shocks of the market system.

Sen is concerned to point to the unevenness with which the benefits of the competitive market are distributed to the individuals involved, and the ways in which this constrains positive freedom for many people. We could examine this in a number of different ways. For example, in Unit 3 Part I, you examined UK statistics on poverty and you saw that they have generated a good deal of debate. The benefits of the market are unevenly distributed across different countries as well as across different regions within a single country. Table 3 shows the extent of differences in Gross Domestic Product (GDP) per head within the countries of the European Union, USA and Japan over the period 1960 to 1994. Figures showing GDP are often taken to be indicative of general living standards. The base for each year is the average of all twelve European countries (less the former East Germany (GDR)); this means that an index number of 100 for any country indicates that the GDP per head for that country coincides with this measure of an average European GDP per head. If a country has an index greater than 100, this means that its GDP is above the European average, whilst a number below 100 means that the GDP is below the European average. In this table then we are able to compare each country's GDP per head with that of all other European countries and the average of all the countries; and we are able to make this comparison for years spanning a period of nearly thirty-five years.

Table 3   European Gross Domestic Product per head (**European 12- = 100**)

	1960	1970	1980	1990	1994 (estimate)
Belgium	98.1	101.9	107.0	104.1	103.8
Denmark	116.5	113.5	106.2	106.2	110.4
West Germany	123.4	117.8	118.2	117.2	115.3
Germany	–	–	–	–	103.7
Greece	34.9	46.6	52.5	47.3	47.4
Spain	58.5	72.6	72.0	75.0	77.9
France	106.3	111.3	113.1	110.7	110.5
Ireland	60.0	58.8	63.1	71.3	78.7
Italy	86.9	95.9	102.9	102.3	104.5
Luxembourg	154.0	138.2	115.9	126.6	132.4
Netherlands	115.8	113.0	108.0	101.9	100.0
Portugal	37.9	47.4	53.0	55.9	59.9
UK	124.0	104.7	97.4	101.4	98.0
12 European countries (excluding former GDR)	100	100	100	100	100
12 European countries (including former GDR)	–	–	–	–	98.0
USA	183.7	159.5	146.9	139.6	141.5
Japan	54.5	89.6	97.2	112.7	118.3

Source: *European Economy*, No.55, Table 9, p.117,1993

In this table we can see that there is considerable variation between the income levels in different countries. For example, looking at the estimates for 1994, the richest country Luxembourg (132.4) has an income level that is nearly three times that of the poorest country Greece (47.4). This disparity is less than the year 1960, where we find that the richest country, again Luxembourg (154.0), had an income level nearly four and a half times that of the poorest countries, Greece (34.9) and Portugal (37.9). Greece's position improved gradually till about 1980 but has declined since that year, whereas the opposite movement is apparent for Luxembourg. The other three of the poorest countries in 1960 — Portugal, Spain and Ireland — have all improved their position over the period. Overall this suggests that there has been a narrowing of income differentials across countries over the period. (It is one of the stated economic and social objectives of EU policy to reduce these disparities and promote a convergence towards high levels of income.) Comparing the USA and Japan with the European countries, we find that both countries were significantly above the European average in 1994. Japan's position has more than doubled over this period from an initial level of 54.5 to 118.3, whereas the USA's position has fallen from 183.7 to 141.5.

In the case of the UK, the per capita income level expressed as a percentage of the European average fell, though unevenly, from 1960 to 1994. This means that in 1960 the average UK income level was 24.0 per cent higher than the average European level, but by 1994 this was estimated to have fallen to a level that was 2.0 per cent below the European average. Whereas the UK level was the second highest in 1960, this had fallen to eighth place by 1990.

If Sen's argument links market transactions with inequalities, we might want to know whether inequalities became more marked during the 1980s with the move towards more market-oriented policies in many countries. There is evidence to suggest that inequality increased during the 1980s in Australia, Austria, Belgium, Canada, France, Japan, the Netherlands, Portugal, Spain, Sweden, the UK and the USA. In most of these countries the changes are small, but in the UK and USA there was a very marked increase in inequality (OECD, 1993).

Changes in the UK distribution of income have been estimated by measuring the percentage of total income accruing to households ranked in five broad groups known as quintile groups, each representing 20 per cent of households. These groups are ranked from the bottom 20 per cent of incomes to the top 20 per cent of incomes. If incomes are distributed absolutely evenly, then each group would receive exactly 20 per cent of total income. In an unequal distribution, the lower quintiles receive less than 20 per cent and the upper quintiles receive more than 20 per cent. The latest figures are shown in Table 4.

Table 4   Percentage distribution of original and final income by quintile group, 1979 and 1992

	1979 Original income	1979 Post-tax income	1992 Original income	1992 Post-tax income
Bottom quintile	2.4	9.5	2.1	6.5
Second quintile	10	13	6	11
Third quintile	18	18	15	16
Fourth quintile	27	23	26	23
Top quintile	43	37	50	44
	100	100	100	100

Note: Totals may not add to 100 per cent because of rounding.

Source: HMSO, Economic Trends, No. 483, pp. 122–3, January 1994.

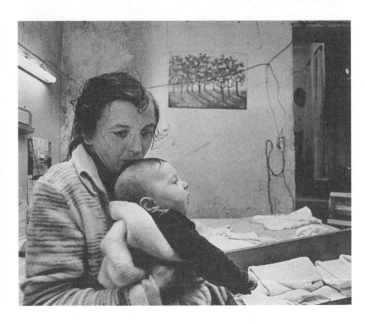

Rich and poor in Europe

Table 4 shows original income and post-tax income for the years 1979 and 1992. Original income includes earnings from employment and self-employment, occupational pensions, investment income and alimony. It provides a measure of household income before any form of government intervention such as retirement pensions or social security. In 1979, the bottom 20 per cent received only 2.4 per cent of total original income whereas the top 20 per cent received 43 per cent. Post-tax income takes account of cash benefits from the state such as pensions and social security, direct taxes such as income taxes and employees national insurance contributions, and indirect taxes such as VAT. The effect of government intervention in the form of taxes and cash benefits is to make the distribution of income less unequal. When we look at post-tax income for 1979, the share going to the bottom quintile has increased from 2.4 per cent to 9.5 per cent and that going to the top quintile is reduced from 43 per cent to 37 per cent.

Comparing 1979 with 1992, however, shows that inequality increased for both original income and post-tax income. The percentage of original income received by the bottom quintile fell from 2.4 per cent to 2.1 per cent, the share of original income received by the second, third and fourth quintiles also fell, while the share going to the top quintile increased from 43 per cent to 50 per cent. The share of post-tax income received by the bottom quintile fell from 9.5 per cent to 6.5 per cent. The shares for the second and third quintiles also fell, the share received by the fourth quintile remained constant, while the share received by the top quintile increased from 37 per cent to 44 per cent. The increase in inequality is the result of a greater inequality in the distribution of original income, and also the reduced redistributive effect of government policies caused by reductions in social security payments together with greater tax cuts for the rich.

The approach to the market that we have been considering in this section emphasizes that the issue of the distribution of economic power is also present whenever we analyse the market and that distributional outcomes may be very unevenly balanced. Although there may be a balance between demand and supply, this approach points out that other dimensions of market societies are out of balance. Building on the income and wealth data that you have already studied in earlier parts of the course, we have looked at some data summarizing inequalities of income and have noted that inequality increased in a number of countries during the 1980s. We examined the evidence showing that the UK became a more unequal society between 1979 and 1992 when viewed in terms of its household distribution of income. These data help to illustrate Sen's argument that economic power is distributed unevenly. They also suggest that one outcome of free-market policies is an increase in the inequality of incomes.

SUMMARY

- Sen's approach argues that the neoclassical emphasis on balance and harmony of interest obscures conflicts of interest and inequalities in market transactions.

- 'Positive freedom' includes access to the resources which underlie the capability to make choices.

- Between the period 1979 and 1992, inequality in the UK increased, and this increased inequality remains even after the equalizing tendency of the tax and benefit system is taken into account.

4.4 UNEMPLOYMENT

The final aspect of the social reformist critique of markets that I am going to look at in this unit concerns unemployment. The social reformist critique of free markets here is that in spite of liberalism's emphasis on the efficiency of markets, the presence of high and continuing unemployment represents a massive waste of human potential and is a moral blight on society.

The first economist to articulate this argument using modern macroeconomic theory was the British economist John Maynard Keynes in his book *The General Theory of Employment, Interest and Money* published in 1936. Until that point, the general opinion was that unemployment was caused by wages being too high. It was argued that the market for labour is just like any other commodity. If there is unemployment with the supply of labour greater than demand, then the wage has to fall — this is the lesson of the neoclassical model of competitive markets, as we saw in Section 3.3. Keynes' criticism of this argument was based on the controversial idea that labour is not just like any other commodity. He argued that reducing wages right across the economy would not reduce unemployment, and that the solution lay in abandoning the idea that markets always result in equilibrium.

Because Keynes was critical about the ability of free markets to produce a high level of employment, he looked to the government of the day to step in with policies to reduce unemployment. From the period 1945 to the end of the 1970s, many Western governments accepted this basic Keynesian message in some degree or other, that is, that they should try to control the level of unemployment. The fundamental Keynesian argument was that the key to unemployment was the level of *aggregate demand*, or the total level of spending in an economy. By increasing aggregate demand during periods of high unemployment, it was hoped to generate extra demand which would be translated into extra jobs. Thus, by increasing aggregate demand when unemployment was high and reducing it when unemployment was low, it was hoped to create the conditions for a stable and continuing high level of employment. To this end, fiscal policy (adjusting the level of taxation and government expenditure) and monetary policy (adjusting interest rates and monetary conditions) were used to influence the level of total spending and ensure a high level of employment.

During the 1980s, however, as we have seen, there was a return to economic liberalism and a rejection of Keynesian thinking. Unemployment, it was argued, was the fault of workers pricing themselves out of a job in the face of fierce international competition, and government had neither the responsibility nor the means to take corrective action. This decade ended with a credit boom and the triumph of free market policies in the UK but, by the early 1990s, recession was evident in many advanced economies and unemployment was once again high on the political agenda. By 1994, about 35 million people — or 8.5 per cent of the labour force — were unemployed in the 24 OECD countries, and it was thought that about another 15 million had either given up looking for work or had unwillingly accepted a part-time job (OECD, 1994, p. 9).

In early 1994 John Kenneth Galbraith, a long-time Keynesian critic of free markets, presented a speech in the UK on the subject of unemployment. This speech is a personal statement which sums up the social reformist approach to unemployment and state interventionism. Galbraith's speech is included in the Course Reader as an example of the social reformist critique that markets are unable to solve the problem of unemployment. Its main argument is that the current high levels of unemployment in even the richer nations are unacceptable, and that governments should take policy action to reduce the unemployment. I would like you to read Galbraith's speech as an example of the social reformist approach to markets and unemployment.

======================== READER ========================
Now read through Galbraith's speech (Chapter 9 in the Course Reader) and make a note of the ways in which his arguments indicate a social reformist approach to markets and unemployment. (Note here that 'underemployment' means the same as 'unemployment'.)

As I mentioned earlier, this speech is very much a personal statement by Galbraith. I found the tone to be one of disappointment that such widespread social and economic problems should still be so evident around the world. It also displays a marked cynicism about individual people's motivation and their lack of concern for those less fortunate than themselves. The social reformism of the speech is evident in the way it is critical of the free operation of markets, and the ways in which it calls upon governments to try to rectify the situation. Did you notice the ways in which it describes the 'enduring equilibrium of underemployment'? This is a direct attack on the neoclassical emphasis on the equilibrium properties of markets. Galbraith is arguing that economies can settle down into an equilibrium situation where unemployment is the norm, and where there are no self-adjusting mechanisms to reduce the unemployment. If this is market equilibrium, he argues, then that equilibrium is not worth having, and governments should intervene to reduce unemployment.

This analysis of unemployment is an argument about the lack of efficiency that characterizes markets, because unemployment involves a waste of human and physical resources. But did you notice the ways in which the speech also refers to the distributional implications of this? Galbraith refers to what he calls the 'deeply impoverished underclass', those who are not able to share in the material benefits and improved life chances that are thought to accompany economic growth in the industrially developed world. This also is representative of a social reformist approach in that it cares about gross inequalities in the distribution of income and looks to government to redress the free market outcome by creating a more equal — or at least a less unequal — society.

Galbraith also refers to a number of specific policy responses by government, such as monetary policy, fiscal action and increased government expenditure. The arguments here are the classic Keynesian arguments for restoring employment by means of an active government policy to increase the level of aggregate demand. These different policies are discussed at length in the following unit which concentrates on macroeconomics and the management of the UK economy, and it develops an extended account of a Keynesian model of the economy. It will explain these different types of government policy in greater detail, examining them critically from different theoretical perspectives. Thus of the three kinds of social reformist critiques of the market outlined in this unit, it is only the Keynesian critique that amounts to a comprehensive model of a system of interrelated markets.

SUMMARY

- Social reformists such as J. K. Galbraith and J. M. Keynes argue that unemployment is endemic and that governments should try to alleviate it.
- The presence of unemployment provides another example of market failure.
- The persistence of high levels of unemployment gives rise to worries about the formation of an underclass.

5   CONCLUSION

In this unit we have examined a number of arguments about competitive markets. Two liberal models of the market were examined where it is argued that the 'invisible hand' of competition leads to outcomes that are beneficial to society as a whole. The Schumpeterian model of creative destruction conceptualizes competition as a dynamic forward-looking quest for innovations in products and processes that will put the corporation ahead of its rivals in the race for market leadership. The neoclassical model of perfect competition (competitive equilibrium) envisages competition as a process where individual firms have no influence over outcomes and where each firm has to take the market price as given. In this case, it is the 'market' as an apparently impersonal force which determines prices and to whose overriding influence all consumers and producers must resign themselves.

In contrast with this liberal emphasis on the advantages of competition, the social reformist critique of markets points to their shortcomings and argues that governments should intervene. The social reformist position accepts that markets are often the best form of economic organization for many areas of economic activity, but it argues that market outcomes are not always efficient and are very often socially unjust. For these reasons, the social reformist is inclined to call upon government to rectify what are seen as the disadvantages of competitive markets. The three weaknesses of markets which I have examined in this chapter are externalities, income inequalities and unemployment.

The debate between liberalism and social reformism is crucial to understanding this debate about the effectiveness of markets and the proper degree of government intervention in the economy. Liberalism tends to be much more sympathetic to leaving market outcomes alone — the *laissez faire* position — whereas social reformism actively campaigns for a wide series of government measures to counterbalance or supplement market pressures. In spite of these differences, however, liberalism and social reformism also share much common ground as social reformism does not want to abolish markets altogether and many liberals also recognize the defects of untrammelled markets. To a certain extent, their differences may be understood as one of degree, with liberals being more appreciative of the advantages of markets whereas social reformists are more impatient with their defects. In terms of specific policy measures, nonetheless, liberals and social reformists often find themselves proposing very different policies, and in the rhetoric of current policy debates these differences loom very large indeed.

Clearly there are different ways of understanding competition, even within a broadly liberal approach to markets. When account is also taken of social reformist approaches, it is clear that there are different ways of understanding the market process, and very different policy conclusions to be drawn.

These issues highlight the close links between theory and policy, between the views that economists take about how the economy functions, and their prescriptions for the role of economic policy. One clear example of this was provided in the area of unemployment: a liberal position would argue that government should not interfere to try to reduce unemployment, whereas social reformism would argue that governments should try to introduce policies that reduce it. In order to understand this debate it is necessary to develop yet another economic model, this time a model of the macroeconomy or the aggregate economy. I have already touched on the importance of the role of aggregate demand for Keynesian models of unemployment. The following unit takes up the story here and introduces you to some models of the macroeconomy, and to the ongoing debate about the best policies for unemployment and inflation.

Summary of two models

	Schumpeter's model of dynamic competition	neoclassical model of perfect competition
model of competition	dynamic competition, that is, forward-looking competition over innovations in products and processes; the process of creative destruction.	perfect competition; at the equilibrium price, demand and supply are equal; firms have no influence over price which is set by market forces.
type of efficiency	dynamic efficiency, that is, innovations arising from technological advances, and economies of scale, result in lower prices and costs.	productive efficiency, that is, prices and costs are at the minimum level given existing technology.
organizational structure	large powerful corporations with their entrepreneurial managers.	firms are small relative to the market they serve.

REFERENCES

Arrow, K. J. (1974) 'General economic equilibrium: purpose, analytic techniques, collective choice', *American Economic Review,* vol.64.

Central Statistical Office (1994) *Economic Trends*, London, Her Majesty's Stationery Office.

European Economy (1988) No. 35, Brussels, Commission of the European Community, Directorate-General for Economic and Financial Affairs.

European Economy (1993) No. 55, Brussels, Commission of the European Community, Directorate-General for Economic and Financial Affairs.

Galbraith, J. K. (1994) *The Economic Question and the Larger Social Scene*, an Address presented at the University of Sheffield, January 27, 1994.

Kay, J. A. (1989) 'Myths and realities' in *1992 Myths and Realities*, London, London Business School.

Keynes, J.M. (1936) *The General Theory of Employment, Interest and Money*, Basingstoke, Macmillan.

OECD (1993) 'Earnings inequality: changes in the 1980s' in *Employment Outlook*, pp. 157–178, Brussels, Organization for Economic Cooperation and Development.

OECD (1994) *The OECD Jobs Study: Unemployment in the OECD Area, 1950–1995,* Brussels, Organization for Economic Cooperation and Development.

Schumpeter, J. A. (1976) *Capitalism, Socialism and Democracy* (first published in the United Kingdom in 1943), London, George Allen & Unwin.

Sen, A. (1989) 'The profit motive' (first published 1983), reprinted in 'The market on trial', *Lloyds Bank Annual Review,* vol.2, pp.106–24, London, Pinter Publishers.

Smith, A. (1976) *An Inquiry into the Nature and Causes of the Wealth of Nations* (first published in 1776), reprinted as vol.2 of *The Glasgow Edition of the Works and Correspondence of Adam Smith,* Oxford, Clarendon Press; reprinted by Liberty Classics, Indianapolis, USA.

Times Newspapers (1992) *Times 1000, 1992–1993*, London, Times Books.

ACKNOWLEDGEMENTS

Grateful acknowledgement is made to the following sources for permission to reproduce material in this unit:

Tables

Table 1: *The World's Top 50 Industrial Companies From The Times 1000* (1993) published by Times Books, London;

Photographs

p.56: (clockwise from top left) British Tourist Authority, Nuclear Electric plc, The Post Office, *Illustrated London News* (22 June 1844); p.81: (top left) Dennis Stock/Magnum, (top right) Dennis Stock/Magnum, (centre right) Erich Hartmann/Magnum, (bottom right) Franco Zecchin/Magnum, (bottom left) Franco Zecchin/Magnum.

STUDY SKILLS SECTION: GOOD WRITING I — SOME TRICKS OF THE TRADE

Prepared for the Course Team by Neil Costello

I would like to go back to the 'Traditions essay' by David Coates (Chapter 22 of the Course Reader) which you have looked at already and to use it to pick up some of the 'tricks' of writing which are used by experienced authors.

You have read the liberalism section in the essay already in conjunction with this unit. I don't want to go back through the whole of that section again but I think it would be valuable to concentrate on part of it and to look at the way in which David Coates tries to keep his readers' interest and the techniques he uses to guide the reader through his work. The Traditions essay contains a lot of difficult ideas but, for me anyway, it is a good read — I find myself drawn through it, my interest is held, I want to know what the next point is to be and although the next point has not arrived yet, I find I am sufficiently aware of what is to come to be able to make sense of the argument when it does arrive. I am not putting the Traditions essay forward as an example of perfect writing. Each of us will have a different view of what that might mean. But I do find David Coates's style accessible and logical with a story line which always seems to be worth telling. It is a good model for us to use in thinking about writing, whether it be course units or tutor-marked assignments, and I think it is worth taking a little time out to see if we can discover how he does it.

The best place to start is *The Good Study Guide*. Chapter 6 of *The Good Study Guide* is about the craft of writing essays, and the section that we are dealing with here is Section 4 — making your essay flow. In that section you are asked to spend a good deal of time analysing the article by Carl Gardner to pull out a number of key points. I suggest that we carry out a similar activity on a short section of the Traditions essay but before doing that you should refresh your memory of the points made in Chapter 6, Section 4 of the *Good Study Guide*.

—————————— ACTIVITY 13 ——————————

Please look back at that section now but don't go through the Gardner article in detail.

Welcome back. Now we need to look at the Traditions essay in the same way. I would like you to turn to the liberalism section in the Traditions essay (Section 2.1) and to look in particular at the short sub-section headed 'Economy and Society'. For ease of reference I would ask you to number the paragraphs; there are 6 in all. What I would like to do now is to go through the same key points you have just read about in *The Good Study Guide*. Remember they were:

- Linking
- Signposting
- Sentences
- Paragraphs

LINKING

Link words and phrases carry the meaning forward from one paragraph to the next. The first word or phrase of each paragraph carries out this task.

The link from paragraph(§)2 to §3 in this section of the essay is carried by the brief sentence describing Adam Smith. §1 had quoted from Smith. Now §2 says in a short sentence who he was and then uses this connection to discuss the period in which he lived.

§2 to §3 is linked by 'for liberal thought ... '. The use of this phrase in this context is the prime link. It is saying that all you have read before is relevant to the point the author is about to make, but that he is going to make a new point, and probably a significant one.

What do you think is §4's link from §3? Have a look before you read on. I think the use of 'this' as the first word of the paragraph is the main link. The *Good Study Guide* comments on the value of 'this' as a link word. 'This' tells you that the subject of the new sentence is whatever was being discussed in the last sentence.

§5 makes its links in a less identifiable way. There are no obvious link words but the first sentence refers to Smith and Ricardo (Ricardo was introduced for the first time in §4) and this contextualises the paragraph and enables the reader to see that a more general point about the whole tradition is now to be made. And that Smith and Ricardo, about whom we have just been reading in the earlier paragraphs, are in some sense representative of this general point.

Finally, §6 has a very clear link: 'For this reason'. This is also a nice example of a link phrase used for arguing., 'For this reason' doesn't just link the paragraphs in a logical way it also indicates that the paragraph to come has its argument based in the points which were made in the previous paragraph. Such links are very useful in moving an essay along.

> ## SUMMARY
>
> As in *The Good Study Guide* what we have been looking at here is the way a writer carries the thread of meaning through a piece of writing by using link words. Each word guides the reader from paragraph to paragraph showing how you should approach the new paragraph in the light of what has been said in the last. This makes any piece of writing flow better, giving the reader a kind of implicit direction sign.

SIGNPOSTING

Signposting is simply a more explicit link. It is important, however. Readers usually need more guidance through an essay than the authors of the essays realise. What might seem as clear as crystal to me in my writing is often disappointingly opaque to my colleagues who comment on it. Put in signposts frequently therefore.

In the short section of the Traditions essay we have been considering there are very few obvious signposts of this kind. This is primarily because I suggested we look at such a short section. The main signpost within the section is the linking sentence in §5. The brief summary of the position of Smith and Ricardo which is found there sets the earlier paragraphs into some kind of historical perspective and the whole of §5 carries out the function of explaining how far we have reached, as readers, and gives us a hint of where we are going, which is then picked up by the phrase 'For this reason' which begins §6.

A good example of a signpost can be found in the first sentence of the next section of the Traditions essay, (Section 2.2 Marxism):

'This is an appropriate moment to pause in our exposition of liberalism ... '

David Coates is signalling why he is moving to a different topic and trying to keep the reader informed and interested in the developing argument. Phrases like this are typical signposting statements and you will find other examples in *The Good Study Guide*.

The need for signposts is summarised like this:

> When you are writing an essay you are taking the reader through an argument. In order to follow your train of thought the reader has to know what questions and issues to hold in mind; in what direction you are heading and why. Readers have their own trains of thought which they are quite likely to follow in preference to yours unless you keep them in close touch with what you are doing. To maintain the thread of argument for the reader you have to pay attention to signalling what is going on. One essential means of doing this is to use link words whose function is to pass the meaning across from one sentence to another and signpost words which tell you where you are in the development of the argument. Some phrases can perform both these functions at the same time.
>
> (Northedge, 1990)

Signposting is an important part of developing the craft of writing.

PARAGRAPHING AND SENTENCES

Paragraphs are clusters of sentences which are all centred on the same basic point. When the main idea or focus changes there should be a new paragraph. Paragraphs can be long or short. Short paragraphs are more punchy and show that the focus of the essay is changing frequently. Longer paragraphs are needed when a particular line of thought has to be argued through.

In the section from the Traditions essay we have been looking at, the paragraphs are all roughly the same length. They are all developing the story in much the same way. It is one of the characteristics of the essay that it uses medium length paragraphs with very little variation. It comes as something of a surprise therefore when a short paragraph appears and this in itself can have an impact on the reader. Look, for example, at the first paragraph under the heading 'Power and the State' in Section 2.2 on marxism. By David Coates's standards this is a short paragraph. It has only three sentences and that fact alone makes the paragraph stand out. It also expresses in a clear way major distinctions between liberal and marxist conceptions of power and the state. No attempt is made in this paragraph to enlarge upon the important point which is being made. It is stated and by being stated so baldly becomes memorable for the reader.

I suspect David Coates did not decide consciously to write a short paragraph at that point. But his experience as a writer gave him the understanding that an important point could be made with some impact through a style change rather than elaborating the point with words. The length of paragraphs therefore also fulfils part of the task of guiding the reader through a piece of writing. Think about varying the length of your paragraphs. The main factor in this should be the 'natural' break in your argument though as a matter of general advice — if in doubt, keep it short.

When we come to sentences much the same kind of advice applies. Sentence length should be varied according to the point which is being made. If the idea is complex you may need a long sentence. If it is a simple point a short sentence is much clearer for the reader. Vary the length of sentences in order to keep the reader's attention and remember that most of us are unable to keep lots of things in our heads all at the same time, so that short sentences are usually better than long complicated sentences with lots of sub-clauses, and other modifying phrases such as the one I have just written and you have just read! If the sentence gets long try to split it in two.

There are a number of good examples of variety in sentence length in the Traditions essay. Look back at the Economy and Society section on liberalism and in particular at §3. The first sentence is short and states the liberal position. The next sentence really emphasises this. Five words: 'It was to be encouraged'. If that second sentence had been longer, and had perhaps explained why it was to be encouraged, it would have had much less impact. The effect of using a short sentence here is to emphasize the point being made dramatically. (The explanation of the point is left to the next sentence, as you can see.) David Coates does not tend to use long sentences. When he does it also has an impact on the way the reader receives the point being made. Look at §5, 3rd sentence, for example. This is a longer sentence built around the optimism of the liberal view and by writing it in this way the extent of the optimism appears bigger to the reader as the sentence itself becomes longer. But, note the careful construction of the sentence, with its structured build-up.

This is a most effective use of the 'tricks of the trade' by a very experienced writer. You can acquire similar skills if you look at the way authors use these tricks and begin to adapt them for your own purposes.

The advice in *The Good Study Guide* is again a good summary for this section:

> The way sentences and paragraphs are put together can do a lot to lead readers through an argument and to bring out its force. Each paragraph does a specific job within the argument of the essay and each sentence makes a specific contribution to the paragraph, but as a writer you have a great deal of scope as to *how* you make them achieve those functions. Sentences or paragraphs can be long *or* short to great effect ... Developing an effective writing style is partly to do with playing around with the effects that can be achieved so that you know how to ring the changes and so keep the focus of your reader's attention where you want it.
>
> (Northedge, 1990)

By studying a short section of the Traditions essay, I have been trying to illustrate how you need to guide your readers through your writing both by using linking words and phrases as signposts, and by the structure of the paragraphs and sentences. I hope you find this brief foray into the way good writing is structured helps you in your own writing. If you have time you could carry out similar analyses of other parts of the course to see how they stand up to scrutiny. If you wish to revise these things or think about them some more, you should perhaps return to *The Good Study Guide*.

UNIT 12   THE MANAGEMENT OF THE UK ECONOMY

Prepared for the Course Team by David Coates

CONTENTS

1   INTRODUCTION

So far in this block we have examined the character of *work* in the contemporary economy, and considered the role of *markets* as key organizing mechanisms of economic life. It is time now to situate work and markets in a wider picture, by looking at the performance of the UK economy as a whole, and at the role of the government as its economic manager.

This shift of focus will enable us to do a number of things. It will help us to fill out an important part of the story of the contemporary UK. It will provide an opportunity to examine some economic theory; and it will provide our first major example of an issue which by Block VII will be occupying us far more — namely the interplay of social science and society. The government plays such a big role in economic life now, and economics looms so large on the political agenda, that we really can't ignore the interplay of politics and economics in our analysis of the contemporary UK. Moreover, since governments have been so influenced in their economic policies by different economic and political theories, it really isn't possible to understand what they have done, and why they have done it, without looking in some detail at the traditions of thought which we first met in Unit 5. And in doing that, we will see that social science can have two impacts, not one. It can help to explain contemporary reality, but it can also at times be one of the forces shaping the reality which it helps to explain.

So I hope that by the end of the unit you will:

1   know more about the ways in which governments recently have tried to manage the UK economy, and about the effectiveness of those attempts; and

2   see how those attempts have reflected different explanations of what goes on in a contemporary economy, and of what can go wrong there — explanations which derive from particular bodies of economic theory.

I hope that three other things will also have happened by the end of this unit:

3   that by then you will have acquired a clearer sense of one of the important ways in which social scientists go about their business: using models to help them grasp the character of complex social phenomena;

4   that you will feel more confident to make your own analysis of current economic policy, by combining your understanding of simple economic models and of broad economic theories:

5   and that you will have a fuller grasp of the ways in which a *public* body (in this instance the government) can shape patterns of *private* activity (in this case the economic activity of individuals and firms).

That is the hope, anyway. I hope that you enjoy the attempt!

2   THE ROLE OF THE GOVERNMENT

Post-war governments in the UK have been heavily involved in the management of the economy. In ways which inter-war governments had not, Labour and Conservative administrations after 1945 accepted that it was their responsibility to achieve popularly-supported economic objectives. For over thirty years after the war, governments of both parties accepted that it was part of their job to do at least four things:

• to maintain a high and stable level of employment

• to achieve economic growth (and rising living standards)

- to keep prices stable, and
- to avoid deficits on the balance of payments.

This post-war economic settlement then gave governments an extensive set of responsibilities of both an internal and external kind. *Internally*, governments attempted to alter levels of consumer spending, the scale and type of public expenditure, the patterns of industrial ownership and investment, and the levels of wages and prices, in the pursuit of economic conditions within which jobs would be secure and living standards could rise. *Externally*, governments tried to influence the rules governing world trade, the shape of trade blocs, and the standing of sterling against other foreign currencies, in order to strengthen the export performance of UK-based producers. And increasingly over time, as that external position of the UK economy weakened, governments sought further internal economic changes to enhance the productivity and competitiveness of local firms in the global market.

This commitment to a competitive and dynamic economy has remained constant down the years, but there has been no such consistency in the policy measures adopted to achieve it. On the contrary, political disputes in large measure have come to turn on just this question: of which sets of economic instruments to use in the pursuit of greater competitiveness. Governments have differed on whether they should:

- alter *taxes and public expenditure* (change what economists call 'fiscal policy');
- alter *the amount of money in circulation* (i.e. change 'monetary policy'): by printing more/less bank notes, by controlling the supply of credit, or by using high interest rates to discourage private borrowing and spending;
- make *legal/administrative changes* (to a whole range of things: taking firms/industries in/out of public ownership; setting up new economic ministries/governmental agencies; limiting pay in the public sector; creating new inspectorates of health and safety at work, and so on);
- arrange *voluntary agreements* between economic actors — say between the TUC and CBI on wage and price restraint; and
- act *internationally*, taking the economy in/out of trade blocs, negotiating bilateral trade deals, borrowing from the IMF, buying and selling foreign currencies to protect the exchange value of the pound.

--- ACTIVITY I ---

We have all been exposed on many occasions to the clash of politicians on economic policy. What we have met less — and what we will explore here — are some of the economic theories which lie behind that clash. But before we do that, it might be useful for you to note down what you think the government ought to do to improve the performance of the UK economy. Then, at the end of the unit you will be able to look back to see if by then your views have changed in any way.

So note down what policies you would pursue, if you had overall political responsibility for the running of the UK economy.

You might like to compare your 'package' of policies with the three packages which have dominated UK economic policy since the war.

Package 1 (in the 1950s) involved little more than the use of fiscal and monetary powers by governments to keep the economy operating as near to full employment levels as possible. Governments (Conservative ones as it happened) just:

- varied taxes (particularly taxes on expenditure), credit limits, and their own spending. In addition they:

- abandoned remaining wartime controls on industry and on incomes;

- maintained a strong pound, and encouraged the Commonwealth as a trading bloc, using sterling as its common currency.

Package 2 (which emerged in the 1960s, and came to fruition in the period of the Labour Government of 1975–79) involved much more government intervention in the economy. Governments still varied taxes, credit limits and their own spending to keep employment high. But they also:

- agreed targets on growth, investment, jobs and wages in negotiations with the CBI and TUC;

- ran extensive incomes policies, trading wage restraint for more welfare provision and union-strengthening labour laws;

- increased the scale of state funding to industry (and even, in the 1970s, took certain firms and industries into public ownership, to supplement those already there from the nationalization initiatives of the 1940s).

The application of this package coincided with a shift in the focus of trade (from the Commonwealth to the EEC, which the UK joined in 1973), and with a fall in the foreign exchange value of the pound.

Package 3 (associated with Conservative Governments after 1979) made something of a retreat from the state intervention of Package 2, and from previously dominant interpretations of the post-war settlement. In the first half of the decade, unemployment was allowed to rise, as part of a policy of industrial reconstruction under market forces. There was

- a retreat from public ownership, with extensive privatization;

- a retreat from incomes policy, which was replaced by tougher labour laws to encourage more market-sensitive wage bargaining;

- a serious attempt was made to restrict state spending and to cut direct taxation and, initially, to control the supply of money; while

- in the second half of the decade, internationally high rates of interest were used to strengthen sterling and curb domestic spending.

(Aspects of the privatization part of this 'package' are discussed in TV06.)

ACTIVITY 2

These three packages are often given labels. The first is often referred to as the *Keynesian* package (because of the influence upon it, as we will see later, of the ideas of John Maynard Keynes). The second, though still Keynesian inspired in part, is often labelled as *corporatist* (a term generally used in political science to indicate regimes which negotiate policy with national representatives of business and labour — negotiate, that is, with key corporate bodies). The third is often referred to as *monetarist / liberal*, because (as again we will see later) it reflected the temporary impact of monetarist economic theory, and the more permanent impact of liberal ideas, on the Conservative governments of the 1980s.

One of the things it might be valuable to do over the next few weeks is to see to what degree economic policy in the 1990s remains broadly Keynesian, corporatist or liberal in inspiration, by putting together your own sketch of government economic policy. You can begin to do this from your reading of newspapers and your watching of/listening to current affairs programmes. I realize that it won't be possible to do too much of this, or even to do it in a very systematic way, because the pressure on your time is already heavy and because, in any case, the information reaching you on contemporary policy will necessarily be rather patchy. But nonetheless there will be information on economic policy in the media and, by taking note of this, you should be able to see at least some of these economic instruments in current use, and to see points of continuity and change in the way governments manage the UK economy.

So, when reading the paper or listening to the news over the next few weeks, try to bear at least some of the following questions in mind:

- *legal powers*: is the government increasing or reducing public ownership? Is it increasing or reducing its regulation of industry, trade and finance?

- *monetary policy*: is the government running a high interest rate policy, or a low interest rate one? What is the pound being allowed to do on the foreign exchanges? Is credit hard to come by, or easy, for industry and private borrowers?

- *fiscal policy*: is the government raising or lowering taxes? Is government spending rising or falling? What is happening about welfare provision?

- *incomes policy*: Do we have one? If not, is the government applying one, *de facto*, to its own employees? What is happening about unemployment?

- *internationally*: Is the government opening/closing the UK economy to foreign manufacturers and to foreign investors? How protectionist is the government being in negotiations *within* the EC and *between* the EC and other trading areas, such as the USA, the Third World or the Soviet bloc?

Another thing we can do is to gather information on the *performance* of the UK economy under all this government management. This will enable us to assess the extent to which the four post-war objectives have been achieved: full employment, economic growth, price stability and a healthy balance of payments. We won't be able to tell from the data whether governments actually *caused* the patterns evident there. Such a causal explanation will be available to us only after we have introduced some theory later on. But at least we will be able see the trends in each of those four policy areas since 1945.

———————————————— ACTIVITY 3 ————————————————

Look at the graph in Figure 1 (on p.102), and note down the periods of apparent 'success' and 'failure' on each of the four policy objectives.

What did you get? It does look as though things went quite well in the 1950s and 1960s. Inflation and unemployment were then low, growth was small but steady, and the balance of payments in most years was just in balance. Indeed, all four indicators seem to move broadly together in those years. But things seem to be a lot more volatile and complicated after 1973. The balance of payments went first into surplus (as North Sea oil appeared) and then into major deficit. As it did so, growth rates moved in the opposite direction, while inflation rose, fell and rose again, and unemployment seemed to settle within a much higher range than in the 1950s. Overall the 1980s, when set against the decade before, seem quite good on growth and inflation, but very poor on unemployment and the balance of payments.

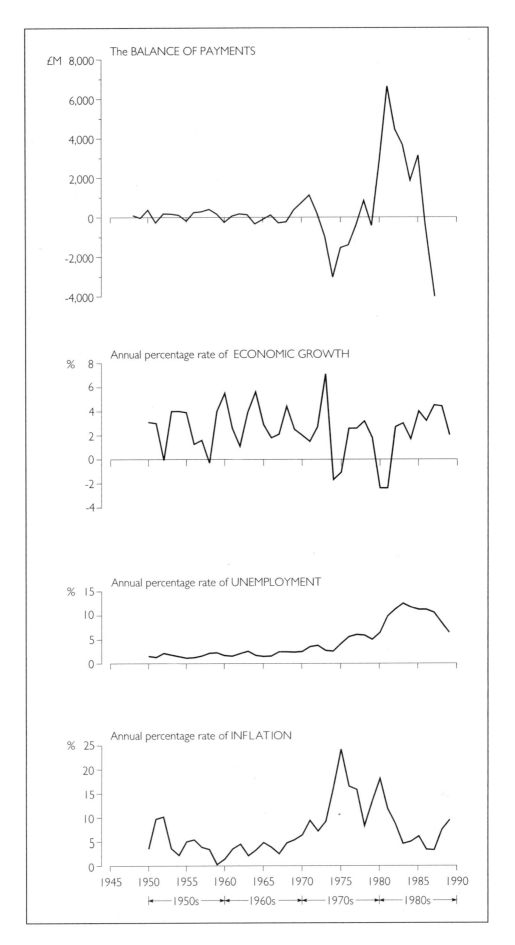

Figure 1

——————————— ACTIVITY 4 ———————————

It is now time for you to update your own inflation index from Unit 3. Go back, price your six items, and fill in the second column of the table in Section 2 of Part 2 of Unit 3. Then take A from B, divide your answer by A and multiply by 100. What is your rate of inflation looking like?

You can perhaps see too that in the 1980s growth rates only improved after a very major recession (between 1979 and 1981); and that the movement in the balance of payments was quite extraordinary: from high surplus in 1981 to unprecedentedly large deficits by the end of the decade. So the performance figures for the UK economy in the 1980s allowed two very different readings: good on growth, if you ignored 1979–81, poor on the balance of payments if you concentrated on the second half of the period. Politicians tended to place the emphasis on different periods, depending on whether their party was in or out of office!

Given the range of interpretations of UK economic performance that it is possible to impose on statistical data of this kind, we would be well advised to seek other ways of assessing the character and quality of what has been achieved in economic terms in the last decade. We can do that, and in the process strengthen our ability to judge the competing claims of politicians, by approaching the whole question of economic performance in *comparative*, rather than in *historical*, terms. For economic performance can be measured in more than one way. It can be measured back over time, as we have just done; but it can also be measured outwards, relative to other similar economies. Look at the statistics in Table 1 for a moment, and then decide what they tell us about the recent performance of the UK economy.

Table 1 Comparative Economic Performance 1979–86

	UK	Germany	France	Italy	US	Japan
Increase in GDP (%)						
1979–86	+10.3	+10.6	+10.0	+12.1	+16.0	+29.0
1979–81	-3.6	+1.5	+1.5	+4.0	+1.6	+8.0
1981–86	+14.8	+9.0	+8.5	+7.8	+13.8	+19.6
Increase in industrial production (%)						
1979–86	+2.8	+7.0	+0.0	+5.0	+13.0	+26.0
1979–81	-9.4	-1.0	-1.0	+3.0	+0.0	+5.0
1981–86	+13.4	+8.0	+1.0	+2.0	+13.0	+21.0
Unemployment (as a % of the labour force)						
1979	5.0	3.3	5.9	7.6	5.8	2.1
1981	9.8	4.4	7.3	8.3	7.5	2.2
1986	13.4	8.5	10.4	11.0	7.0	2.8
Inflation (% per annum)						
1979	13.4	4.1	10.8	14.8	11.3	3.6
1986	3.4	-0.3	2.6	5.8	2.0	0.4

Source: Maynard, 1988, p.95.

Here the performance begins to look rather different. Unemployment and inflation rates are higher in the UK in the 1980s than in most of the other countries included in the table; and the UK rate of growth compares unfavourably with growth rates in Italy, the United States and Japan — if the period taken is the longer one, 1979–86. But the UK growth rate looks better if the shorter time span 1981–86 is used instead. The depth of the 1979–81 recession here was greater than elsewhere, but so too has been the rate of recovery.

So once more it looks as though the 1980s was a better decade for UK economic growth than it was for UK unemployment, this time when judged comparatively as well as retrospectively. But the inflation performance now doesn't look quite so good as it did a moment ago; and there is still that ominous deficit on the balance of payments (in Figure 1).

From the graph on the balance of payments (Figure 1), would you expect that the share of world trade in manufactured goods captured by UK-based producers to have gone up/gone down since the Second World War?

It has in fact gone down. It had fallen from 25.5 per cent of world exports of manufactures in 1950 to 9.3 per cent by as early as 1975 (Alford, 1988, p.15); and by 1983 the UK had become a net importer of manufactured goods for the first time since the industrial revolution. Governments in the UK since the Second World War seem not only to have managed the economy with increasing difficulty, but to have presided over a diminution in the role of UK-based manufactures in the global economy. As we turn now to try and explain the pattern and effectiveness of UK economic management since 1945, we will have to bear that shrinkage in manufacturing in mind too.

3   MODELS AS AN AID TO UNDERSTANDING

I want us now to turn to address the question of how to make sense of that complicated pattern of government policy and economic performance. With so much going on, how can we explain it all? How indeed can we even begin to put such an explanation together?

I think that we can best begin the pursuit of that explanation by recognizing our limitations, by being quite clear that we just can't hope to make sense of all this complex detail at one go. But there is nothing unusual about this. On the contrary, social scientists often face such a problem: the danger of being 'swamped' by too much information, too many variables, too complicated a set of interconnections. And a characteristic and very valuable response is to stand back from the complexity for a while, choosing instead simply to abstract from that complexity just part of what's going on, for examination first. Inevitably that means that analysis begins (though it will not end) in a very simplified way. There is great virtue — in social analysis — in starting with the simple and moving to the complex, and that is what I would like to do here.

So one way of reaching an understanding of all that complexity is to start with a simple model that captures some key elements of the overall picture. Then, later, we can work our way back towards the complexity from which we began, but only once the simplified picture has been grasped and understood. If we do that, of course, then our choice of 'model' becomes critical; and our problem here is to know which one to choose.

We looked at three possible contenders way back in Section 6 of Unit 2. There we laid out three explanatory frameworks, three big models of the world economy: one that divided the world into traditional and modern societies, one that split the world into North and South, and one that split it into core and periphery.

--------------------------------- ACTIVITY 5 ---------------------------------

If those three models are now only a vague memory, go back and take a quick look at Section 6 of Unit 2. You won't need the detail. Just glance at the three diagrams there, and at the summary at the end of the section, to refresh your memory on the general character of the models being used.

Those three models have one great strength and one great weakness for our purposes here. Their strength is the emphasis they place on the *global* context of local economic activity. They remind us that no economy is an island, cut off from the rest of the world. Instead they oblige us to question the character and local impact of the relationships *between* economies. But what they don't do is offer us much guidance on how to grasp the character of the economies themselves. The models are so global in their focus — they paint the picture so wide — that they leave the internal workings of the local economy unclear. Yet it is those local workings we want to explore now. So, without losing contact with the question of the global economy raised by the models in Unit 2 (we will come back to it in the last section of this unit), we need to find a model that starts at the other end of the economic process — starts locally — one on which we can build out towards an understanding of the way local and global forces shape economic life here. A number of such models are available to us. The one that we will use for the bulk of this unit treats the economy as a series of flows of resources and expenditures. Let's see what use we can make of it in the pursuit of our understanding of the pattern and impact of government attempts to manage the post-war UK economy.

BUILDING A MODEL OF THE ECONOMY

At its most elementary, it helps to think of the economy as a series of exchanges between two key economic institutions: between households (which among their other functions, provide labour power and consume products) and firms (who employ labour, and make products). The households supply workers to the firms and the firms supply goods and services to the households. We can draw that set of exchanges as Diagram 1. The shaded square denotes the area of the economy. The boxes denote the key economic institutions, the arrows the exchange between them.

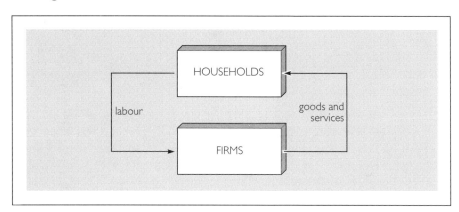

Diagram 1

At the same time, spending flows round the circuit in the opposite direction. The firms pay the households wages for the labour they supply, and the households pay the firms for the goods they obtain from them. We can draw that as Diagram 2, with the flows of expenditure shown as broken lines.

But life of course is not so simple. Banks and other financial institutions get into the act, as households deposit money with them, and as they lend money to

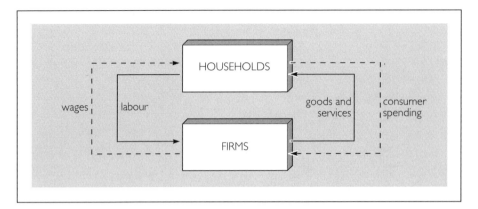

Diagram 2

firms, and to other households. The firms then use that money (and some of their income from the sale of goods and services to households) to buy machinery and raw materials from other firms — firms who don't themselves sell anything directly to households. We can draw that too (see Diagram 3).

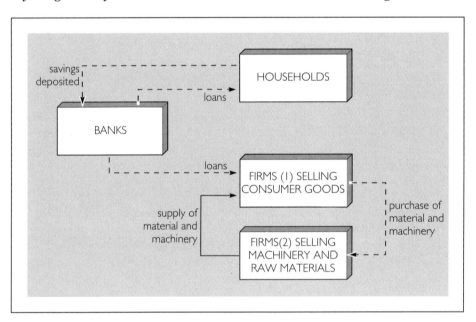

Diagram 3

The government is in there as well, taxing some households and paying benefits to others, and taxing some firms and spending money with others (see Diagram 4).

Perhaps you are beginning to see that we could easily make each of these flow diagrams a lot more complicated. We could add a flow of taxes from firms to government in Diagram 4, for example, or firms' deposits with banks in Diagram 3. But our simplified diagrams are capturing some of the important exchange flows at work in the contemporary UK economy; and if we overburden them with detail they will begin to lose their clarity. That is a common trade off in modelling: the loss of complexity in the pursuit of clarity. So let us keep it simple for a moment, and add some of the flows associated with foreign trade. We will draw it with households doing all the buying of imported goods, and firms all the exporting — just to keep it simple. In truth, of course, both firms and households engage in foreign trade — buying foreign goods and (in the case of firms at least) selling things to foreign consumers. In each case money goes in one direction, goods and services in the other — to give us a picture of the kind shown in Diagram 5.

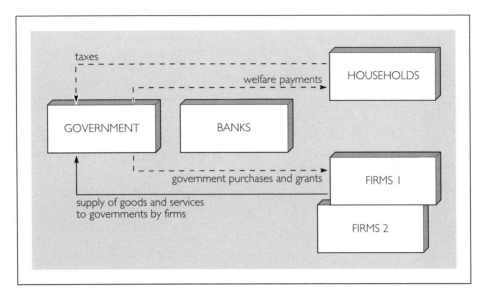

Diagram 4

You should notice here that, for the moment, we have left 'foreign buyers and sellers' totally unconnected with the banks and firms of the UK economy. In Diagram 5 the complex interconnections between the local UK economy and the global one hardly surface at all. The linkages between UK firms and multinationals, the international linkages of the money markets, the close relations between governments — all that is for the moment left to one side. We will look at Diagram 5 in considerable detail — and make it more complex — towards the end of the unit, when we have used the simpler version to clarify government economic policy within the UK itself.

Armed with these diagrams, let's go back to the government's economic policy objectives. The four policy commitments adopted after the Second World War, you may remember, were as follows:

. high and stable employment

. rising living standards

. price stability and

. a healthy balance of payments.

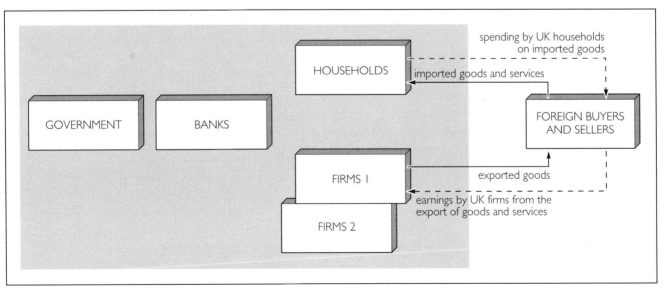

Diagram 5

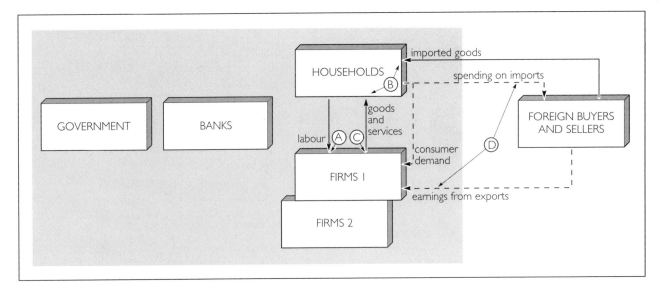

Diagram 6

Let's fit each of these to the exchange flows we have isolated so far (see Diagram 6).

- *High and stable employment* requires that the flow of labour called to the firms is large enough (and remains large enough) to absorb as many as possible of those who want to leave the household to obtain paid employment. That flow of labour can be seen at point 'A' in Diagram 6.

- *Rising living standards* require that the flow of goods from the firms to the households steadily increases over time (that flow, of course, can include imports). The flow is marked at point 'B' in Diagram 6.

- *Price stability* is more difficult to capture in Diagram 6, because the diagram shows movements in resources rather than changes in price. But for the moment it is enough to note on our diagram the point at which any price inflation will first manifest itself. That is at point 'C'. Price stability requires that the price of goods and services leaving the firms remains as unchanged as possible.

- And *the balance of payments* requires that spending on imports does not outstrip earnings from exports (point 'D' in Diagram 6).

So when the government manages the economy with those four policy goals in mind, it has to influence the full set of money and resource flows to obtain a satisfactory result at points 'A', 'B', 'C' and 'D' in Diagram 6. The question, of course, is how.

SUMMARY

- Models help us to begin to understand complex realities by extracting key relationships for separate study.

- A model of the national economy can be built by isolating flows of resources and expenditure from firms to households, between banks and firms, in and out of the public purse, and between local economic actors and foreign buyers and sellers.

- Such a model can be used to locate the flows of resources and expenditures that governments must influence in the pursuit of particular economic objectives.

4   THE MANAGEMENT OF THE ECONOMY

The answer to the question, 'how should the UK economy be run?', has varied over time, as bodies of economic theory have risen and fallen in popularity in government circles. Fashions here have been dictated partly by which issues were uppermost in the minds of politicians and the electorate. In the 1940s and 1950s, with memories of inter-war unemployment still firmly in mind, the prime concern of policy was full employment. In the 1960s and 1970s, as international competition intensified, attention shifted to the balance of payments and economic growth. In the 1980s, attention moved to inflation, and the commitment to full employment took more of a back seat. The benchmark of government economic success in the 1950s was the level of unemployment. By the 1970s, it was the rate of economic growth. A decade later, it was the rate of growth of the price index; and that shift of benchmark coincided with a shift too in the focus of policy itself. In the 1950s governments concentrated, as we saw at the start of the unit, on the management of levels of *demand* in the economy. By the 1980s, politicians had come to see how important it was too to influence levels of *supply*. We can trace that shift of emphasis by looking at the rise and fall of particular bodies of economic theory.

4.1   THE MANAGEMENT OF DEMAND

The most influential set of answers available to policy makers in the first twenty-five years after the Second World War derived from the writings of John Maynard Keynes. His general position is discussed in the Reader article on traditions of thought, so please turn to that before reading on.

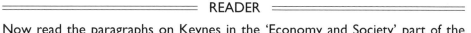

=== READER ===

Now read the paragraphs on Keynes in the 'Economy and Society' part of the Social Reformism section of Chapter 22 in the Course Reader (especially pages 282–4).

The orthodox view of how to solve unemployment in the 1930s was to leave it to market forces. Markets — as we saw in the last unit — will in the end 'clear' if the prices of the goods handled within them respond to the demand and supply conditions evident in the market place. But such a view — of long term solutions to unemployment that involve reducing wage levels in the labour market — did not satisfy Keynes. He wasn't convinced that wage cutting and reductions in government spending would bring the economy out of depression. Instead, he believed that what the economy required — in conditions of mass unemployment at least — was an increase in *Aggregate Demand*, not a reduction.

Let's pause for a moment to clarify this notion of 'Aggregate Demand'. If you look back to our earlier diagrams, you will see that we have already introduced some of the component elements of total/aggregate demand in the economy.

1   In Diagram 2, we introduced spending by households on goods and services (a flow often known as consumer demand or 'c').

2   In Diagram 3, we introduced spending by firms on machinery and raw materials (often known as investment demand or 'i').

3   In Diagram 4, we introduced spending by governments ('g'); and

4   in Diagram 5, we introduced the amount earned from exports ('x') less that spent on imports ('m').

These are the component elements of demand in the economy; and often appear in economics textbooks as:

Aggregate Demand = c + i + g + x - m

Keynes argued strongly that the task of increasing Aggregate Demand fell to government. If governments wanted firms to flourish, jobs to expand and living standards to rise, then they had to *increase* the flows of demand in the economic system. Look at the position of the firms in our diagrams, and at the flows reaching them. If they are to employ more people, they will need more income coming into their coffers, with which to pay the extra workers. The diagrams suggest a number of sources of income for the firms.

No doubt as the economy expands, all of these sources of income for the firms will grow; but the expansion has to start somewhere, and the question is where. Keynes's answer was broadly as follows (see Diagram 7). That the expansion would *not* begin with:

- *exports* (flow 1). It is obviously desirable to sell more abroad; but it is very hard to guarantee such a growth in exports from within the UK itself. Governments can encourage industrial efficiency in UK-based firms, but even so levels of demand abroad depend on many factors over which UK governments have no direct control. Nor would it begin with

- *consumer demand* (flow 2). This was exactly what Keynes wanted to increase. If it went up, firms would sell more, employ more people, pay out more wages, and so expand further. But there was, and is, a real chicken and egg problem here. More wages won't be paid out until consumer demand has already gone up (or until some aspect of the total demand experienced by firms has risen). The process of expansion cannot therefore start here. As Keynes said in 1930, 'you cannot start the ball rolling in this way' (Clarke, 1988, p.115). Nor can it start with:

- *investment goods* (flow 3). This too was something that Keynes wanted to see expand. But he realized that firms would only buy new machinery if they had confidence in the future profitability of their operations. That confidence could be improved if the cost of borrowing was low — which was why Keynes favoured a policy of low interest rates. But he also realized that banks wouldn't lend to firms who couldn't sell their extra output; and that firms wouldn't seek extra funds until they too could be sure of new markets. So business had to be stimulated by the creation of an environment of economic expansion; and for that stimulation Keynes looked to the government.

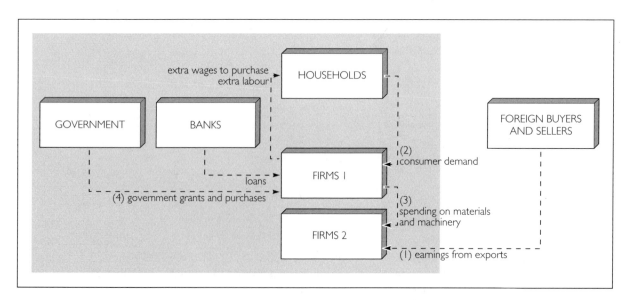

Diagram 7

- *government spending* (flow 4). This was the key entry point for Keynes and for other Keynesian-inspired economists: for the State to use its own spending to generate new demand in the economy, and to alter tax rates to free the private spending of others. We had to spend our way out of recession, and use the revenues generated by that expansion to pay off the government spending which had precipitated it. Such government spending would have a *multiplier effect* throughout the whole economy, as the expenditure and income initially released passed from hand to hand, generating income on each occasion, so overall providing an increase in the volume of total demand far in excess of the original government injection — and stimulating new investment and production in the process.

─────────── ACTIVITY 6 ───────────

This notion of the 'multiplier' is easiest to grasp in a simple game. Gather five friends and one pound in cash (in the form of five 20p pieces). You be the government, injecting a pound into this economy, and let your friends save 20p whenever the money reaches them. Now inject your pound by spending it with your first friend. Her income will go up by £1. She will then spend 80p of that pound with the next friend. That friend will have an extra income of 80p. That friend will then spend 60p with friend No. 3. Friend No. 3 will spend 40p with friend No. 4, who will in turn spend 20p with friend No. 5. Your original pound will have generated a total income of £1 (friend 1) plus 80p (friend 2) plus 60p (friend 3) plus 40p (friend 4) plus 20p (for friend 5). That is £3.00 in total. Not bad for one pound injected. That is the multiplier!

SUMMARY OF KEYNES ON UNEMPLOYMENT

- Keynes (and even more strongly, his followers) suggested a key role for the government in the economy: as a manager of total demand.

- To obtain economic growth and full employment, the government needed to increase Aggregate Demand, and to avoid the wage-cutting, public-sector retrenchment strategy often canvassed in government circles.

- The quickest way to increase demand was to increase government spending, and allow that spending to flow round the economy: generating (as it did so) employment (and hence more wages and higher consumer demand) and greater business confidence (and thereby more investment by firms).

4.2   KEYNESIANISM IN PRACTICE

British governments in the post-war years were economically active in ways which seemed to meet well the role anticipated for them in Keynes's *General Theory*. From 1944, as we have seen, they accepted a commitment to full employment, and from even earlier (it is conventional to cite the 1941 budget as the first occasion) politicians in power used both fiscal and monetary techniques to keep economic activity as near to full employment as they could manage. As we saw in the summary of policy earlier, they used fiscal techniques (alterations in taxes) to influence purchasing power. They also influenced money flows through the banks by the scale and character of their own borrowing, and by altering the terms on which private credit could be obtained. Overall, governments superintended a quite unprecedented peace-time growth in the scale of their own spending, and in the provision of bank credit to private borrowers; and as the years passed government activity in the economy became increasingly vital to the processes of private investment there. When state activity was greatest — in 1975 — 57.9 per cent of the Gross National Product passed through its hands. Of that 57.9 per cent, 28.3 per cent was only transfers by state agencies (such as the social security system) from one person to another, but the rest (26.9 per cent of GNP) was resources actually directly consumed by public bodies such as hospitals, schools, the police and the army. For in the years after 1945, governments became major employers in their own right. 7.2 million people worked for central and local government, the nationalized industries and the armed forces in 1975; and many more, in private industry, were dependent on the government for the purchase of what they produced, for the regulation of the conditions under which they worked, and even for the investment on which their jobs depended (Coates, 1984, pp.219–20).

Academics still disagree about whether all this did, or did not, constitute a genuinely Keynesian revolution in economic policy after the war. But at least there can be no doubt that the politicians responsible for these policy changes invariably thought of themselves as Keynesians. And well they might. For they were prepared to stimulate private investment as Keynes had suggested they should, and, with very few exceptions, they all seemed to have absorbed the very Keynesian assumption that it was the government's responsibility to manage the economy in the pursuit of full employment. Governments of all political persuasions in Britain in the 1950s and 1960s seem to have recognized that the total level of demand in the economy could be too low to persuade firms to employ everyone who wanted a job, and that it was the government's responsibility to alter the level of total demand in order to keep employment levels high.

So the impact of Keynesian ideas on government policy in the first twenty-five years after the war is clear. It is also clear, however, that the impact of those ideas diminished over time: and that the 1970s and early 1980s witnessed something of a counter-revolution in economic theory and policy against what had become by then the ruling Keynesian orthodoxies. That revolution was fuelled by the emergence of two difficulties for Keynesian-inspired policy makers, difficulties which for a while eroded both public and professional support for Keynesianism.

The first of those difficulties arose out of the *local–global* tension in economic policy to which we referred in Section 2. The second arose out of the altered relationships between the *public and private* in the modern economy associated with the implementation of Keynesian policies. Let's take each difficulty in turn.

DIFFICULTY NUMBER 1

Ask yourself what happens after the government has injected spending into the economy, if local industry is less efficient than its foreign rivals?

The answer to that question points to a major long-term weakness in Keynesian solutions to unemployment. Keynesianism has no monopoly of this weakness, as we will see later. The difficulties created by the lack of international competitiveness of UK-based industry were evident from the 1880s, and remained into the 1980s, long after Keynesianism had been formally abandoned as the source of economic policy. But the lack of competitiveness of UK-based manufacturing firms first re-surfaced as a problem after the war in the era of Keynesian dominance, and indeed helped to bring that dominance to an end. So its impact needs to be understood first as a source of difficulty for Keynesianism.

For if locally-produced goods are more expensive, or of poorer quality, than similar goods produced abroad, then it is not unreasonable to suppose that export earnings will fall (as foreign consumers buy fewer UK-made goods) and that the amount spent on imports will rise (as home consumers buy better foreign-made products). Then if the government allows levels of internal demand to rise, instead of local jobs being created, foreign ones will be created (as much of the extra income will literally 'leak out' of the system as spending on imports). Governments in such situations will therefore not just face problems of local unemployment. They will also face a *balance of payments* problem.

This certainly happened in the UK in the 1950s and 1960s. Governments tried to implement Keynesian policies of demand management; and as they did so, they increasingly ran into balance of payments difficulties. Indeed this recurring balance of payments problem was *the* way in which successive British governments in those years — and their Keynesian-inspired economic advisers — became aware of the diminishing competitiveness of UK-based industry. They kept running into balance of payments deficits — in 1955, 1960, 1964, 1965 and 1968 — deficits which were small by comparison to those of the late 1980s, but which at the time were deemed large enough to require a governmental reaction.

Governments reacted initially by concentrating on the immediate payments crisis. Only later did they begin to probe seriously for underlying causes. As they did so, economists and politicians of a broadly Keynesian persuasion put together what we might term a Keynesian explanation of the competitive decline of UK-based industry. Their understanding of this issue developed through a number of stages.

1 Their first characteristic reaction to the balance of payments crises, as we have said, was to *slow down demand* (in policies known at the time as 'stop-go'). They increased taxation and reduced their own spending.

2 Then they began to see the problem as one, not of demand alone, but of the *trade union power* which seemed partly to generate it. They began to see that twenty-five years of full employment gave workers and unions the confidence to negotiate high wage and income settlements: and that these high wages added to industrial costs and inflated levels of consumer demand. In such a situation, all Keynesian-inspired governments could do, whilst struggling to maintain full employment, was to seek wage restraint — either voluntarily through agreement, or statutorily by imposition — in effect throwing a barrier across the inflated wage flow (at the line 'X–Y' in Diagram 8). We can illustrate that on our flow diagram. Follow the sequence of points 1, 2, 3, 4 and 5.

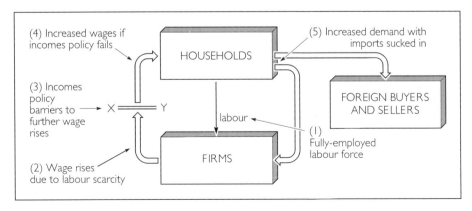

Diagram 8

3 Here indeed was one major reason for the supplementation of demand management by direct negotiations with trade unions in the 1960s and 1970s. While employment was high and trade unions strong, governments needed voluntary agreements with union leaders and members to restrain money wages and to keep costs down, if they were to avoid the build up of inflationary pressures: and for this reason stop-go policies were supplemented with incomes policies, one after another between 1961 and 1979.

4 The realization grew too that 'stop-go' was itself a problem — that this *persistent blocking of demand* was a serious disincentive to investment. Many Keynesian economists saw low levels of investment in manufacturing plant and equipment as the key to the UK's relative economic decline, and explained that as a consequence of a general lack of reliable and expanding levels of demand in the economy. Such a view encouraged many of them to urge a rapid expansion of the economy, in the hope that investment would surge in volume in response to easier selling conditions. It also encouraged Keynesian-inspired economists of a more left-wing predisposition to advocate direct government action to stimulate investment even when market incentives were low: action in the form of indicative planning in the National Economic Development Council, or (more radical still) direct government investment in industry and infrastructure. They began, that is, to suggest government action on the *supply* side of the economy, as well as the *demand* side.

—————————————————— ACTIVITY 7 ——————————————————

Let's pause for a moment to clarify this notion of the 'supply side' of the economy, since the term is often used these days by politicians and political commentators. Run your eye back over Diagrams 1–5. Can you see any flows of resources supplied into the economy by firms or households? I can see four:

1 the supply of labour from households to firms;
2 the supply of goods and services from firms to households and government;
3 the supply of machinery and raw materials from firm to firm; and
4 the supply of exports from UK-based firms.

These flows make up the *supply side* of the economy. When politicians talk of 'supply side problems' they mean problems in the quantity, quality and price of labour, and in the price and availability of the goods and of services produced by that labour. They also mean, of course, the conditions of production that create such problems of supply in the economy: the quality of its technology, its working practices and its ability to produce efficiently goods and services that are in demand.

———

5 Keynesian-inspired analysts also increasingly recognized that the quality of 'demand management' here couldn't constitute the entire explanation of any inadequacies on the supply side of the UK economy. After all, virtually every government in the leading capitalist economies was using similar policies, and they weren't presiding over increasingly uncompetitive manufacturing sectors. So why 'we' were doing so badly then came to be explained by the interplay of a series of ultimately *non-economic* factors: things such as poor education, inadequate management, entrenched class divisions, unregulated industrial relations, and an amateur civil service. This list in its turn inspired many of the reforms of education, industrial relations, the civil service, and the training system pursued by governments in the 1970s.

> ## SUMMARY OF KEYNESIANISM ON THE DECLINING COMPETITIVENESS OF UK-BASED FIRMS
>
> - Keynesian-inspired economic thought was slow to see the problem of the declining competitiveness of UK-based industry; and met it first simply as a balance of payments problem.
> - The initial Keynesian-inspired response was directed at reducing demand in various ways, culminating in a series of incomes policies.
> - Increasingly however, Keynesians came to see that deeper problems of economic uncompetitiveness existed, whose resolution required extensive social and industrial reform, aimed at improving the supply side of the British economy.

DIFFICULTY NUMBER TWO

This inability of Keynesian-inspired governments to improve the UK's economic performance might have been enough to undermine the general credibility of Keynesian ideas in political circles in the 1970s. There certainly was a moment in the late 1960s when Keynesianism seemed available as an explanation of *unemployment* but not of *relative economic decline*. What finally undermined the dominance of Keynesianism however in the 1970s was the sudden reappearance of mass unemployment as well.

———————————— ACTIVITY 8 ————————————

This second face of the crisis of Keynesianism can easily be grasped if we go back to our flow diagrams again, and re-examine what we have established so far. Ask yourself this question. If there is unemployment, what does Keynesianism suggest that governments should do?

Your answer?

I hope it is 'increase demand', 'most easily by increasing government spending'. Now what happens if you increase demand too far — that is, if you put into the system more income than can easily be satisfied by the purchase of UK-produced goods and services? What happens if all UK workers are employed, and there is still excess demand in the system?

Your answer?

———

This is more difficult. As we have seen, imports will be sucked in, with balance of payments consequences; but in addition the general price of all goods will probably rise. You will get *price* inflation.

It should be said that Keynes himself was well aware that inflationary pressures could grow as full employment was reached, and that he was quite cautious in his own estimates in the 1930s of the level of unemployment at which governments should *stop* increasing demand. Many of his followers however eventually shed that caution, and felt the economy could be run at very nearly full employment before inflation would occur. For them, there was no conflict between inflation and unemployment. One would arrive only as the other departed. But by the late 1950s even they had come to see that inflationary pressures could build up before full employment levels had been attained — that in fact what they faced was a trade-off between unemployment and inflation in which the control of inflation required them to run the economy at less than full employment. That was in itself something of an intellectual retreat by Keynesians; but at least through the 1950s and 1960s Keynesian economists and the governments they advised experienced that trade-off as one between *low* levels of unemployment and *low* levels of inflation. As we saw in our earlier graph, prices rose at most by 5 per cent a year in the 1950s and 1960s, and normally by much less; and unemployment averaged just 2 per cent in the First World as a whole. Governments in Britain experimented with incomes policies, and with 'stop-go' cycles of economic expansion and contraction, to keep unemployment and inflation in balance and at a low level.

The age of Keynes can be said to have ended abruptly in the 1970s when economic crisis (in the form of a dramatic increase in the level of unemployment) returned; and to have ended with Keynesianism itself in crisis because suddenly rapid inflation and high levels of unemployment were occurring *together*. Some commentators dubbed this 'stagflation' (a mixture of *stag*nation and in*flation*). Stagflation was not supposed to happen in a world of Keynesian economics; and initially Keynesianism had no effective policies to deal with one of its faces that would not, at the same time, accentuate the other.

──────────────── ACTIVITY 9 ────────────────

To consolidate this point, it is worth noting down an example of something a Keynesian-inspired government might do if it wanted to create jobs by increasing total demand in the economy. Now write down what that government would have to do to the same thing if it wanted to reduce inflation.

What did you write down? There are lots of examples to choose from, of course. I thought a government wanting to increase purchasing power might raise child benefits without adding to taxation elsewhere. But if it wanted to cut inflation, that is the last thing it could safely do. Such a government wanting to solve unemployment and inflation together would be really stuck.

Not surprisingly, this impasse precipitated a very serious crisis in Keynesian economics. Keynesian suggestions just didn't seem to work any more. At least, they didn't seem to work with the degree of success they had enjoyed in the 1950s and 1960s. This was the second face of the crisis of Keynesianism. The first face (the difficulty of solving the UK's relative economic decline) weakened the credibility of Keynesianism here. But this second face (the re-appearance of mass unemployment and inflation in all the major western economies) produced a more generalized retreat from Keynesianism among economists and state planners everywhere.

4.3   THE MANAGEMENT OF SUPPLY

The strengths and weaknesses of Keynesianism remain a major issue in contemporary economic theory, and are indeed one of the reasons why contemporary economics is such an exciting area in which to work — big theoretical debates have re-appeared to break the consensus on Keynesian policies that characterized much of the discipline in the 1950s and 1960s. These days economic texts often start with lists of some of the available 'schools of thought'. The one in front of me (Roger Backhouse's *Macroeconomics and the British Economy*) starts, as we will do here, with the clash between Keynesianism and Monetarism, though it is quick to stress that in reality 'there is a much greater diversity of thought than is suggested by this division ... for there are many economists who fit into neither category' (Backhouse, 1983, p.2). Eclecticism is now very much the order of the day among many professional economists. They borrow bits and pieces from a number of 'schools of economic thought', to come to their own particular position on questions of economic policy.

I emphasize that because we lack the space here to follow the detailed contours of this debate between schools of thought. Second and Third level courses are the place in which you will be able to read that material if you wish to do so. All that I can do here is to suggest to you that, although the detail of contemporary debate in this area ebbs and flows between a number of eclectically-constructed positions, the centre of gravity of the anti-Keynesian position was originally — and largely remains — a monetarist one. There are few 'pure' Keynesians left in the trade these days; and not many 'pure' monetarists. But debate still oscillates in large part between these 'pure' positions; and it is hard to grasp the contemporary debate without some grounding in them. So to round out our understanding of contemporary economic policy choices, let me lay out for you a broadly *monetarist* explanation of the problems facing those who would manage the UK economy back to competitive health and full employment.

READER

The intellectual origins of Keynesianism lay in social reformism, as we saw earlier. Those of monetarism are largely *liberal*. In Unit 11 we asked you to read Section 2.1 the 'Liberalism' section of Chapter 22 of the Reader. If you have difficulty recalling what you read then, it might be worth just refreshing your memory by quickly re-reading that section now.

The 'liberal' legacy to modern day anti-Keynesian economists is at least two-fold: a faith in the capacity of markets to act as economic allocators, and a belief in the capacity of individuals to act rationally — within markets — to maximize their own self-interest. As the Reader article suggests, and as we discussed at greater length in Unit 11, liberal economists tend to believe that markets will pull the supply and demand for goods and services into harmony (into equilibrium, as economists would say) if prices are allowed to rise and fall undisturbed by government regulation; and that individuals are capable of adjusting their behaviour in a rational way in the light of all the information that is available to them. From this viewpoint, Keynesian management of the economy – far from being a good thing – is an 'interference'. It both disturbs the market's capacity to generate an optimal equilibrium of demand and supply, and sets up new pressures on individuals rationally pursuing their own self-interest. These are disturbances and pressures which will produce, not economic growth and full employment, but ultimately economic stagnation and price inflation. The legacy of Keynesian demand-management, on this view, is a diminution in the *supply* of goods and services generated by UK-based firms and entrepreneurs.

The broadly 'monetarist' critique of Keynesian economics goes as follows:
- The only secure guarantee of long-term full employment lies in the existence of efficient and competitive firms. So if governments concentrate on managing the level of demand in the economy, and ignore difficulties of supplying goods to meet that demand, their attempt to produce full employment will fail. All that will happen is that a gap will emerge between demand and supply, so creating inflation.
- The risk of such an inflationary gap is particularly great if governments try to push unemployment down below its 'natural level'. Monetarists believe there is a necessary residuum of unemployment whose level is determined, not by levels of demand, but by local standards of training,

degrees of job mobility, levels of trade unionism and other 'blockages' on the free movement of labour. If governments use increases in demand to push unemployment below that level, labour will become scarce, wage rates will rise, and the general level of prices in the economy will be forced up. If politicians really want to get the residuum of unemployment reduced, they ought to direct policies instead at the supply-blockages — at trade union power, barriers to job mobility and so on.

- When prices levels are rising rapidly, and particularly when they are rising more rapidly here than in competitor economies, business confidence in the viability of investment projects will weaken, because the market-strength of local business will be undermined and because trade unions will begin to demand wage settlements which *anticipate* future price inflation. The resulting diminution in business confidence and industrial competitiveness will then produce unemployment. So getting rid of inflation is the real key to job protection, and demand-management of the Keynesian kind is not.

- Indeed Keynesianism actually makes things worse, and has become a major cause of unemployment in its own right. For Keynesianism means big and active government. It means high taxes, lots of regulations, plenty of welfare provision, and generous subsidies to firms. All this is a serious disincentive, so the monetarist argument runs, to efficiency and private initiative, and hence to the creation of an adequate supply of goods and services. Welfare provisions, if too generous, stop labour coming forward at a proper price. Subsidies to firms encourage industrial inefficiency. What Keynesianism does, according to monetarists, is to encourage government to 'over govern'; and by getting in the way, governments actually block the supply of goods from the private sector on which in the end non-inflationary economic growth depends. Far from being a solution to unemployment and economic recession, Keynesianism, according to monetarists, has become part of the problem.

- The solution to inflation (and through it to high levels of employment) is therefore for the government to refrain from detailed economic management. For as we saw in Unit 10, governments cannot — on this argument — create 'real' jobs. Private firms do that. All governments can do is to *create the conditions* in which firms can expand: and it is on that task, and on that task alone, that they ought to concentrate.

Monetarism as a school of economic thought gathered its name from its belief that the prime task of government was to *control the supply of money*. Initially many monetarists argued for a close and relatively quick relationship between money supply and inflation. Cut one and the other would fall. However, that didn't happen in the 1980s, and economists sympathetic to monetarism became more aware than once they had been that the link between money and inflation was much weaker, and less reliable, than they had originally thought. So these days monetarists come in many shades and colours, and at one border of the 'school' slide away into positions close to Keynesianism. But the stronger the monetarist they are, the more they remain preoccupied with the control of the money supply as the key to price stability, economic growth and full employment. Monetarist-inspired economists remain wedded too to what we can call a general *liberal* stance on the use of market forces to improve the supply of goods and services in the economy. It is a stance that prefers private economic activity to public regulation. It is a stance that wants labour markets to operate without political interference or trade union monopoly power. It is a stance which is unhappy with government initiatives in the areas of welfare or industrial aid, initiatives that soften the impact of market forces on individual companies and individual workers. It is a stance, that is, which believes that governments govern best that govern least.

Overall therefore we can say that the reappearance of a broadly monetarist presence in contemporary economic debate in the 1970s and 1980s marked the return of liberal views to a political agenda otherwise dominated since 1945 by social reformist ways of thinking and acting. It is monetarism's roots in a liberal preference for markets over governments which help to explain why the 'rolling back of the state' became *the* watchword of monetarist thought in the 1970s, and its ultimate solution to the unemployment and inflation that was initially so perplexing to economists of a more Keynesian hue.

SUMMARY: MONETARISM ON UNEMPLOYMENT

- Monetarists reject Keynesian concentration on demand management as the key to full employment, and emphasize instead free markets, supply-side questions and the importance of stable prices and controlled supplies of money.

- Monetarists see Keynesianism as part of the problem — creating barriers to the efficient supply of goods and services by 'over governing'.

- Monetarists therefore argue for a rolling back of the state, and a prioritizing of the struggle against inflation, as the way to solve unemployment.

———————————— ACTIVITY 10 ————————————

Set this summary against that for Keynesian policy on unemployment (page 109). Can you list the differences between the two approaches?

I hope that your answer indicates big differences in their concerns (unemployment for the original Keynesians, inflation for monetarism), in their focus of policy (on demand, on supply), and on their attitudes to government spending (big and small respectively).

This re-assertion of a liberal commitment to self-regulating markets, and its associated critique of social reformist 'interference' in market processes, then prepared the way for a monetarist explanation of why the manufacturing sections of the UK economy had become progressively less competitive over time. They had suffered, we were told, more than comparable economies elsewhere, from an excess of economic management. They had experienced too much Keynesianism.

1   Monetarists pointed to this 'excess' as a general tendency of all Keynesian-inspired democratic politics. There were votes to be won by short-term economic tinkering. Politicians promised jobs, but produced inflation. They over-heated the economy, and so reinforced the capacity of strong trade unions to extract high wage settlements. They also spent too much as governments, and in this way fuelled inflation directly. In other words, what was missing — according to monetarists — from the original flow diagrams with which we explained Keynesianism was the 'political weight' provided to the households as voters by the experience of full employment and rising living standards, to supplement the 'industrial muscle' given to trade unions by the same. If we now bring back our flow diagram from the section on Keynes, we can amend it in the following way.

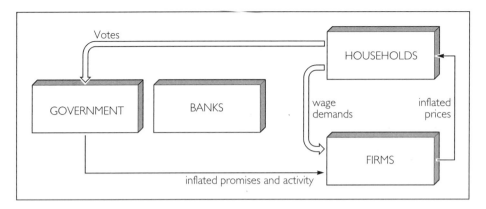

Diagram 9

2   Not all countries however were equally susceptible to this political conse-quence of Keynesianism. Their 'vulnerability' varied with the strength of their labour movements, the electoral success of Labour parties, and the particular legal codes surrounding trade unionism. From a monetarist perspective, UK-based manufacturing firms have been particularly prone to dwindling competi-tiveness because of the particular strength here of these pro-Keynesian forces, as enshrined in the post-war settlement which obliged governments to main-tain full employment at all costs.

3   The political dominance of Keynesianism in the UK then triggered dwin-dling competitiveness; because

(a)   UK-based firms faced by strong trade unions inside their factories and high demand in the economy around them, couldn't easily alter their labour practices and so modernize their productive systems to meet that demand. Instead an inflationary gap opened up, greater than that experienced by their international competitors. ￢

(b)   Capital was exported out of the UK, and not invested here, because rates of return were higher abroad, in economies where labour was cheaper and indus-trial modernization easier to implement; and this set up a 'vicious circle' of economic decline, where low investment in the UK left productivity and profits low here by international standards, and so deterred local investment still further.

(c)   Excess demand in the UK economy was quickly mopped up by imports from more efficient foreign producers, whose better quality and lower-priced goods destroyed local firms (and hence local jobs) and created balance of pay-ments problems. If governments then held interest rates high here, to attract in foreign funds to cover the resulting balance of payments deficit, that just made life even tougher for local firms, who invested less and became weaker still in international terms.

On this argument, the continual decline in the competitiveness of UK-based industry could not be avoided without dramatic changes in policy and a painful period of re-adjustment. Monetarism, like Keynesianism before it, then sug-gested a political programme. In principle there is no reason why economists convinced of the importance of the supply of money in the creation of inflation should all subscribe to the 'package' which follows. But many influential monetarist economists did (and still do); and the logic of their argument, and its roots in a liberal tradition of thought, explains why. They favour reductions in government activity in the economy, and a strengthening of markets (by the denationalization of publicly-owned concerns and reductions in trade union legal rights). They are prone to advocate tax reductions and the removal of regulations on working conditions or wages — which they see as a barrier to work, saving, enterprise and efficiency; and they want industries to rationalize and modernize under the stimulus of competition.

SUMMARY: MONETARIST EXPLANATION OF THE DECLINING
COMPETITIVENESS OF UK-BASED INDUSTRY

- Dwindling competitiveness, according to monetarists, derives from excessive government involvement in the economy, and from the associated strengthening of trade union legal rights.

- Social factors may have played a part in that economic decline, but the root problem is really a political-economic one, namely Keynesianism itself.

- The solution to relative economic decline lies in the restructuring of industry under the full force of international market forces, the rolling back of the state as an economic actor, and the dismantling of the post-war political settlement.

───────── ACTIVITY 11 ─────────

Compare this summary with the explanation inspired by Keynesianism, and given in summary form at the end of Section 4.2. Then fill in the following chart.

	Keynesianism	Monetarism
Causes of unemployment		
Causes of declining competitiveness		
Solution to unemployment		
Solution to declining competitiveness		

(We will come to my suggestions for your answers here in the conclusion to the unit.)

───────── READER ─────────

Now read Chapter 10 in the Reader, 'British economic growth over the long run' by Nick Crafts. This should give you a feel for the kind of literature produced by economists in this field.

Both the density of Crafts's style, and his careful approach — testing first one factor and then another — are typical of how many economists go about their business. You will find Crafts concentrating on supply-side problems without subscribing to the entire monetarist package. Look in particular at Section II of the Crafts article — the section headed 'The Post-1945 Economy in Historical Perspective'. Notice how Nick Crafts builds his argument, paragraph by paragraph, examining in turn:

Paragraph No:

1 the performance of the UK economy relative to its competitors;
2 levels of government spending — and the Bacon Eltis thesis we met in Unit 10;
3 the impact on economic performance of a particular type of trade unionism in the UK;
4 the way trade unionism is joined by other causes of low productivity: poor training, low levels of technical skills, and inadequacies in education;
5 political barriers to tackling supply-side problems in the immediate post-war years;
6 politicians' preference for demand management in the 1960s;
7 the way mergers failed to raise productivity or stimulate more research and development;
8 the adverse impact of low productivity on investment levels;
9 the dwindling share of trade in manufactured goods captured by UK-based firms in the post-war period.

As a final task on the Crafts' article, look at the remaining section (on the Thatcher Government's economic reforms), and ask yourself 'what supply-side blockage gets most attention in the Crafts's article?' I think you will find it is trade union power, and the associated need for industrial relations reform. Keep this in mind, for comparison later with Marxist explanations of the dwindling competitiveness of UK-based manufacturing industry.

4.4   CONTEMPORARY POLICY OPTIONS

If we now go back to our flow diagrams once more, they will help us to place much of the current controversy in economic management. As we have already seen, Keynesian economists in the 1950s and 1960s advocated the stimulation of demand by the government as the key to economic growth and full employment. We can mark that on the flow diagram at point 'A' on Diagram 10. Later Keynesian positions, as we have also seen, emphasized the importance of incomes policies as a way of heading off wage-led inflation. That we can mark at point 'B'. The thrust of monetarism, on the other hand, was to curb government spending (at 'A') and to cut taxes (at 'C'), to free a greater supply of labour to (and commodities from) a revitalized private set of firms. These tax cuts (though falling on households) were seen by monetarists as inspiring a more bountiful supply of labour and enterprise, which in their turn were supposed to generate a greater quality and volume of output from firms.

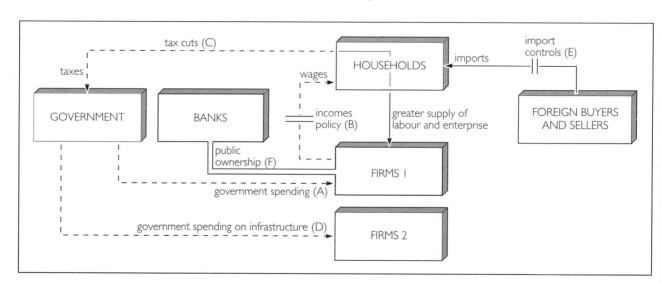

Diagram 10

But when Conservative Governments in the early 1980s implemented policies of an apparently monetarist hue, they still ran into balance of payments problems, and seemed incapable of squeezing inflation out of the system. The money supply proved hard to define and even harder to control, so that 'by 1985–6 effective monetary targeting was virtually abandoned' (Maynard, 1988, p.131). Attempts to stimulate the supply of goods and services by cutting taxes also inflated levels of consumer demand; and the decision in 1979 to remove barriers to the free export of capital initially produced just that — an outpouring of capital from the UK. This exported capital then earned lots of interest payments in foreign currency, but still made no direct contribution to the stimulation of output and employment at home; and, indeed, by 1990 the Conservative Government was having to run a policy of high interest rates – to attract foreign investors back into the UK and to dampen down levels of consumer demand (particularly for imports). Yet these same high interest rates also made investment by UK firms more expensive to finance and meant that only projects yielding a very high rate of return were worth undertaking; so that, as in previous decades, the protection of the balance of payments seemed to be in tension with the expansion of the manufacturing base.

In consequence, by 1990 a supposedly monetarist-inspired government was open to the charge that it had returned to old-fashioned Keynesian-style demand management, and had still not presided over a supply-side miracle capable of guaranteeing long-term employment and prosperity for all. In their defence, ministers often pointed to the unbroken sequence of economic growth which followed the slump of 1979–81; but they were still vulnerable to two kinds of criticism:

- that they had not been monetarist enough; or
- that what was required now was a 'supply-side Keynesianism'.

The first of these criticisms should be intelligible to us. The call went out for yet greater retrenchment of government policy at points 'A' and 'C' on the flow diagram. 'Supply-side Keynesianism' however may be less clear. It derived its force from the assertion that during the:

> Thatcher era a great deal of productive capacity had been scrapped and there had been relatively little investment in new plant and equipment. As a result manufacturing industry was now operating fairly close to full capacity such that, without renewed investment, there was only limited potential for a rapid Keynesian style of reflation.
>
> (Rowthorn and Wells, 1987, p.315)

So this time the call for an increase in demand in the UK economy was focused — not on tax cuts to boost consumption — but on heavy government investment in industry and in industrial infrastructure. This would involve government action at point 'D' in the diagram. Supply-side Keynesianism was (and is) often accompanied by a number of other proposals: namely to re-introduce incomes policy (at point 'B') to stop wage-led inflation; or (in more radical versions) to use import controls (at point 'E') to prevent adverse affects on the balance of payments; or even (in more radical versions still) to extend public ownership to the banks and big corporations to ensure compliance with such expansionist policies (at point 'F').

In effect we now face a spectrum of proposals for the management of the UK economy that we might label as:

pure monetarism	mild monetarism	orthodox Keynesianism	supply-side Keynesianism

These of course coincide with a political spectrum that runs from the right wing of the Conservative Party through the Centre parties and out to the Labour Left.

————————————————— ACTIVITY 12 —————————————————

Now read the following extracts, which are from policy proposals around in the late 1980s, and see how you would place them on the spectrum we have just been discussing.

1   *Andrew Glyn*

Under present economic conditions, in the UK and the world economy, a successful 'Plan for Employment' requires effective controls over all foreign exchange transactions, trade, prices, credit, and investment. It is impossible to see how these can be imposed without public ownership of the credit system and the subjection of all major companies, by one means or another, to thoroughgoing democratic control and management. This must include statutory rights for workers in the planning of priorities for the economy, in the management of enterprises and in the running of their workplaces.

(cited in Coates and Hillard, 1987, p.141)

2   *John Smith*

The UK's manufacturing tradable capacity must be restored in such a way as to allow a resumption of economic growth at socially acceptable levels of unemployment and output. The first problem is therefore how to raise the volume and quality of investment that producers are willing to undertake. The second is how to ensure that sufficient financial, human and other resources of the right amount and quality are available for the programme of investment and innovative activity required. The first and over-riding requirement in raising the volume of private sector investment is to raise the level of effective demand for domestic manufactured output ... Private sector investment will not be forthcoming without the prospect of a period of sustained buoyant demand. Ensuring a high and sustained level of demand by raising capacity utilization (and as a consequence raising profit margins) is therefore a necessary requirement for industrial investment revival ... Necessary though demand expansion is, it cannot by itself be sufficient ... [since not simply the volume but also] the efficiency with which ... investment is allocated and used is also of great importance. It is in this connection that an active industrial policy as part of a planned domestic reflation can make a difference ... Planning can help ... [to ensure] that in every case we ... sustain three engines of recovery. These are investment, research and development, and training.

(ibid, pp.46–50)

3   *The Institute of Directors*

Lower public spending, tax cuts, removal of rigidities in the labour market and elimination of administrative and legislative disincentives to business growth represent the only viable policy for medium and long term economic growth and job creation. Increased public spending would weaken business confidence at home and confidence in financial markets abroad; it is the primary cause of employment levels lower than the economy would otherwise generate ... Research shows that tax cuts have a better effect on job creation and price inflation than the alternatives of cuts in national insurance contributions, increases in public spending or marginal employment subsidies.

Capital spending on roads or infrastructural renewal, although desirable, is among the least effective means of increasing the number of permanent jobs.

Suggestions that tax cuts would be spent on imported domestic consumer goods are in many ways a counsel of despair; and the steepest rise in import penetration since 1980 has been in capital goods, bought by industry, rather than consumer items.

Wage Councils should be abolished because they stifle job prospects for many young and part-time workers.

(ibid, p. 223)

4   *Patrick Minford*

Our proposals ... are for substantial falls in taxation, paid for by wide-ranging reduction in the responsibilities of the state through the privatization of virtually all state production, of state consumption of goods that are not 'public', and of some transfers (notably pensions). To protect the poor at work, we propose a negative income tax (health insurance, education and pension contributions would be compulsory) ... We also propose to restore jurisdiction of the common law to all union actions (i.e. withdrawal of all immunities), [and] to ... render closed shop agreements ... null and void.

Wage Councils and wage regulations should be suspended as their terms run out. Small businesses should be effectively exempted from all labour protection laws.

... The qualifying period for workers to enjoy their rights under the Employment Protection Act should be raised to five years; and workers should be allowed to contract out of these rights. Health and Safety rules should be advisory, and industries should be self-regulatory on these. Benign neglect should be shown by the executive arm of the state towards other laws in this general area.

The solution to the problem [of insufficient mobility of labour between regions] lies in simultaneously liberalizing the private rental market and eliminating council house rent subsidies, while limiting (via benefit capping) the amount paid to the unemployed.

(ibid, pp.267–9)

What did you decide? It seems to me that the four extracts are printed here in the reverse order to the policy spectrum cited above. They each contain claims that are highly contentious (about such things as the kinds of tax cuts which work best and so on), so they all need to be treated with caution. But they can at least be placed on our spectrum. Andrew Glyn's argument (associated with the Campaign Group of Labour MPs) is a radical version of supply-side Keynesianism. John Smith, at the time a front bench Labour spokesperson, offers a milder version of Keynesianism, though still with supply elements visible within it. The Institute of Directors are mildly monetarist, Patrick Minford more 'purely' so.

Finally, look back to the first Activity in this unit, when you indicated your policy preferences. Do they sit on this policy spectrum? If so, where? Do you want to change any of your policies in the light of what you have read?

5   A MARXIST READING OF THE UK ECONOMY AND ITS MANAGEMENT

So far we have stayed, in our theorizing on economic performance and decline, within the confines of mainstream economics — operating within an intellectual universe bounded by *liberalism* and *social reformism*. Now it is time to step outside; to examine a marxist reading of the same thing.

===================================   READER   ===================================

Please read the 'economy and society' part of Section 2.2 on Marxism in Chapter 22 of the Reader.

Can you see now that marxists expect capitalist economies to be in perpetual difficulties: competing with each other, constantly changing their production systems, forever displacing workers, creating unemployment and poverty of a relative, if not always of an absolute kind? What marxists are not so good at explaining is why, for twenty-five years after the war, mass unemployment did not occur. If monetarists have a sort of answer to the question of why Keynesianism ran into difficulties in the 1970s, marxists need one for why those difficulties took so long to appear. And marxist economists, like everyone else in this debate, also need to explain why, in the struggle between competing capitalist economies, it is the manufacturing section of the UK economy which has progressively lost out in that competition.

To get to grips with all that, we require a different model. The flow diagrams used in the unit so far create a picture of an economy in which already-produced commodities and money are exchanged between households, firms, banks and governments. By their very constitution and use, the flow diagrams suggest that the difficulties faced by state economic managers ultimately rest in these processes of *exchange*. We have already seen that many Keynesian and liberal economists have now gone beyond this focus on exchange and demand, to look at questions of supply. What we need to emphasize now is that, in addition, our model's preoccupation with processes of exchange does not sit easily with many marxist approaches to contemporary economics. Many marxist economists are willing to concede that economic difficulties manifest themselves in the sphere of exchange, but they insist that their origins lie elsewhere, in the processes of *production* from which commodities emerge — in the social processes, that is, which take place before exchange can begin.

Our flow diagrams do not include that production process, and in that way help to shut out a consideration of marxist positions. To grasp these, we will therefore need a different model, one that can grasp production as well as exchange; and we will also need some sense of the relationship between this new model and the flow diagrams we have used so far. One way of visualizing that relationship is to think of the flow diagrams as resting — as perhaps they actually are as you read this — flat on the top of the desk/table at which you are working. Marxists suggest that, beneath the table, social processes of production go on, processes which eventually throw up onto the table's surface commodities to be bought and wage-earners to buy them. Underneath the table (underneath the flow of exchange relationships) a circuit of production goes on, one that can be illustrated in a different diagram (see Diagram 11 opposite).

According to marxists, the circuit of production in a capitalist economy starts at point 'X', with capitalists spending their money on the purchase of machinery, raw materials and labour power. That labour power is then set to work on the materials and machinery to make commodities — in this instance, chairs — which are then sold. So long as the sale of those chairs realizes more money than the original sum released, the capitalists make a profit, and the circuit of production can begin again.

As each circuit of production follows from the one before, marxist economists expect that the volume of machinery being used to produce chairs will actually grow (as individual capitalists, obliged to survive by out-competing each other, do so not simply by working their own labour force harder and longer, but also by giving them better and better equipment as well). So over time, on this argument, the proportion of labour to machinery in the circuits of capitalist

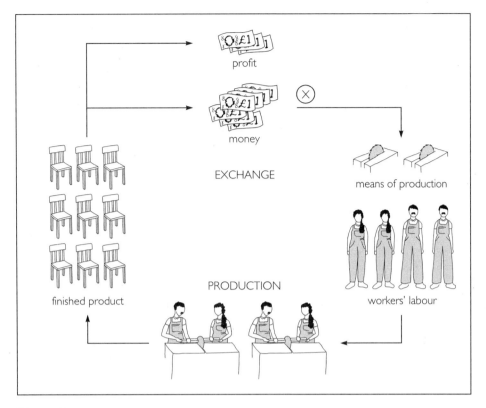

Diagram 11

production necessarily shifts towards machinery. This is what produces economic growth, by adding to the stock of capital locked up in production. But at the same time this expansion of the capital stock threatens the rate of profit on which the continuation of economic growth depends. For with more and more capital tied up in production, capitalists need more and more profits to make the whole exercise worthwhile. It was Marx's view that the generation of more and more profits could not be sustained indefinitely as the balance between labour and machinery shifted in the economy as a whole. It was his belief that, over time, employers would find it harder and harder to squeeze the necessary volume of profits out of their diminishing work forces; and that in consequence crises would occur because of a tendency for the rate of profit to fall.

Such crises in the cycle of production occur, according to marxist economists, when the whole cycle fails to produce enough profits to fuel the next cycle. That is, *crises occur when profits collapse*. Now profits can collapse within the cycle at two points. Marxists argue that capitalists meet problems at times in *selling* what they produce. They do so because the workers lack the purchasing power to buy all the commodities that their labour produces; and lack this purchasing power necessarily because capitalists cannot pay workers enough. They have to hold back some money as profits. Each individual capitalist has both to keep wage costs down, and to keep prices as high as can be managed. Capitalists can therefore make goods but cannot always sell them. They cannot 'realize' their profits. When working-class purchasing power is too weak, capitalism experiences a *crisis of realization*. It is to this kind of crisis that Keynes was reacting in the 1930s. Such a crisis manifests itself at point 'A' on the circuit of production in Diagram 12.

Profits collapse too when workers are strong. But then the problems arise at the point at which commodities are *made*, rather than at which they are sold. Capitalists cannot then work their labour force hard enough to extract a sufficient surplus from them, nor pay them low enough wages to leave a satisfactory margin of profits. The ratio between what capitalists pay their workers and the

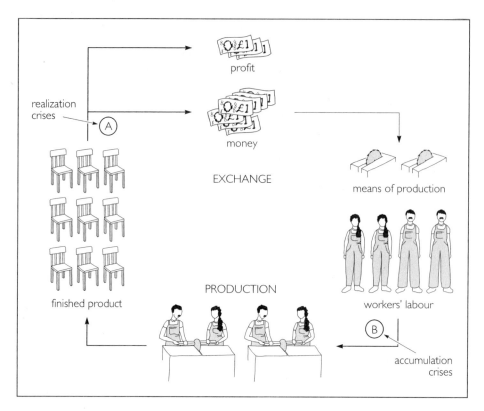

Diagram 12

value of what they produce is too low to generate profits on a scale sufficient to fuel another round of investment and production. In these circumstances capital does not 'accumulate'. The system has a *crisis of accumulation*. This occurs when the working class is too strong. It manifests itself at point 'B' on the cycle of production. One such crisis occurred in the 1970s.

Marxists believe that this tension will never go away until capitalism does. If attacks on trade unions and working-class living standards go too far, local firms will find it difficult to sell their goods. That is why even monetarist-inspired governments have in the end to expand local demand. But when they do, they run the risk of strengthening local working-class industrial power, with all the consequences that has for local competitiveness. So the management of the economy never finally 'succeeds'. Governments just ride the tiger, and will carry on doing so through the 1990s.

SUMMARY: MARXISTS ON UNEMPLOYMENT

- Marxists believe that unemployment derives from a tendency in capitalism for profits to collapse.
- Marxists expect capitalism always to contain this potential for crisis. It is not the likelihood of crisis which varies, only its form.
- The form the crisis takes depends on the strength of class forces surrounding production: realization crises when the workers are too weak, accumulation crises if they are too strong.

So marxists are sceptical of the long-term effectiveness of the policy measures that we have discussed in the earlier parts of this unit. They believe that the deep-rooted differences of interest between capitalists and workers will not go away; and that because they will not, governments will always find themselves trying to balance unemployment and inflation, profits and wages.

Yet it is clear that such a balancing act is easier to perform successfully in some periods than in others (after all, in retrospect, even in the UK the long post-war boom between 1948 and 1973 was a period of sustained growth, high employment, and only slowly rising prices). And it is equally clear that such a balancing act has been easier in the post-war period for some countries than for others. The Japanese economy in the post-war years has experienced spectacular rates of economic growth. So too has the West German economy; and neither has seemed as beset as the UK with problems of unemployment, inflation and balance of payments deficits. Let us see how marxist economists explain all that.

They do so by deploying their understanding of capitalism not as a system of markets, as liberal thought would have it, but as a system dominated by a competitive struggle between individual capitalists, and as a system driven by fundamental cleavages of interest between capitalists and workers. In other words, they handle the question of the performance of this economy against that of another by talking about 'social classes'. They concentrate on *the balance and character of class forces* in particular societies, examining the way in which, in each society, capitalists compete with one another and with their work force. The critical feature of the UK economy to which marxist economists have recently drawn attention, as indeed have many of their non-marxist colleagues, is the competitive weakness of local manufacturing firms. They have also been disputing among themselves as to whether to root that weakness in features of the capitalist class in the UK, or in features of the relationship between capital and labour. There is an on-going debate within marxist economics and economic history about whether the weakness of UK-based manufacturing capital has been caused primarily by the strength of other sections of the capitalist class (in this instance finance capital, the City) or by the strength of non-capitalist classes (in this instance the working class, organized in trade unions). In other words, marxist economists have argued that UK industry has declined relative to its competitors in the post-war years either because the City has been too strong or because the trade unions have.

================= READER =================

To see the detail of that argument, now turn to Chapter 11, in the Reader, 'Theories of economic decline in the UK' by Bernard Stafford.

To help you with this article, let me indicate what I take to be the main points of each paragraph in turn.

ParagraphNo:

1   Here Bernard Stafford emphasizes the common concern of marxist analysts with class relationships but their disagreement about the relative importance of two such sets of relationships: those between different sections of the capitalist class, and those between capitalists and workers.

2   The argument that emphasizes the importance of relationships within the capitalist class is associated with the writings of Eric Hobsbawm. The Hobsbawm thesis is that: as international competition intensified towards the end of the nineteenth century, British industry retreated into the protected markets of the Empire rather than modernize. British capital shifted its focus from industry to trade and finance. Industrial interests within the capitalist class lost out to mercantile and financial interests.

This second paragraph is long but important. It draws attention to three important features of contemporary economic life in the UK. These are: (a) the propensity of big UK-based firms to base their production overseas; (b) the limited involvement of UK banking in the financing of UK industry; and (c) the capacity of financial interests to shape government economic policy to the detriment of industry. Trade union power is noted, but treated as of only secondary importance. Instead, the weakness of the manufacturing sector is explained as the product of a shortage of investment funds (the rest having been exported) and of government policies — on things like interest rates — designed to protect the international position of the City/sterling.

3 and 4 The next two paragraphs show that this kind of analysis pops up all over the place, including in an essay of mine. (So it must be right!)

5   In fact Bernard Stafford doesn't agree. He favours the alternative argument that competition between capitalists and workers holds the key to the declining competitiveness of UK-based industry. Kilpatrick and Lawson, who have put this case most persuasively, stress that trade unions are stronger at factory level in the UK than in other competitor capitalisms, and have been since the end of the nineteenth century.

6   They argue that this local union strength has had an adverse effect on the level and growth of industrial productivity.

7   They also argue that it has triggered a cumulative process of economic decline. The retreat into imperial markets was a product of that decline, not its cause.

8   The Hobsbawm thesis and the Kilpatrick and Lawson one are — we are told — quite incompatible.

SUMMARY: MARXISM ON THE DECLINING COMPETITIVENESS OF UK-BASED INDUSTRY

- Marxists see the relative weakness of UK-based manufacturing industry as a consequence of the balance of class forces in UK industry and society; but disagree about whether finance/labour are the most important barrier to manufacturing competitiveness.
- One view of the dwindling competitiveness of UK manufacturing locates its cause in the overseas orientations of the financial section of the UK capitalist class, and in the influence that section of the class has had on government economic policy.
- The other view stresses the strength of trade unionism at factory level, compared to the strength of unionism elsewhere, and sees that as the cause of a cumulative process of decline.

So it is possible to build an even wider continuum of explanations of unemployment in the UK, and of the relative decline of UK manufacturing, than we possessed previously. To the Keynesian and monetarist explanations and solutions we summarized earlier, marxist ones can now be added.

Table 2 Summary table

	Keynesianism	Monetarism	Marxism
Causes of unemployment	Deficiencies in demand	Excessive government intervention in the market	Tendency of profits to collapse
Causes of declining competitiveness	Under-investment caused by shortages in demand and lack of social reform	Too much Keynesianism, 'feather bedding' industry and labour	The balance of class forces in the UK (between sections of capital/between capital and labour)
Solution to unemployment	Government 'management' of the market	The 'rolling back of the state'	No permanent solution under capitalism – only amelioration to alter the 'form' of the crisis
Solution to declining competitiveness	Government-led social and industrial reform	Opening of the economy to the full force of international competition	No easy solution once 'fallen behind' in the competitive struggle – so go for socialism

6   CONCLUSION: THE GLOBALIZATION OF THE LOCAL ECONOMY?

As perhaps you can now see, there is a considerable overlap between some marxist and some non-marxist explanations of the dwindling competitiveness of UK-based manufacturing industry. Kilpatrick and Lawson emphasize the power of trade unions. So too does Crafts. Hobsbawm focuses on the banking system. So too did the Wilson Committee mentioned in the Crafts article. There is similarity of argument at times; and there is similarity of approach. The entire debate on UK economic decline is necessarily a *comparative* one. The local economy is in decline, if it is, because of differences between the way things are done here and the way they are done abroad. There is necessarily a global dimension to any discussion of the strengths and weaknesses of the contemporary UK economy.

Now it will be interesting to see if that dwindling competitiveness persists into the 1990s, or whether it was 'solved' by Thatcher government initiatives in the decade before. If you are a non-marxist, and particularly if you identify strongly with the economic policies of Conservative governments, it is presumably possible for you to believe that the UK's economic problems will go away. But what will not go away is the existence of foreign economies and the impact of international forces on economic activity within the UK. On the contrary, as many marxist and non-marxist economists have recently argued, there are strong indications that such international economic forces will become more important as the years pass. And if they are right, then in the 1990s we will need economic models which recognize the centrality, to economic life here, of the interplay of the local and the global. We will not be able to make do with models that look at the UK economy alone. Indeed it is possible to list a number of recent changes in the global economy whose presence now calls into question the adequacy of models of the economy that treat economic life here as somehow isolated from any global context. That list would have to include:

- The emergence of *multinational corporations*, particularly since the 1960s, and the way they dominate production in key sectors of the economy (in motor vehicles, computers, electronics and so on).

- The associated establishment in the UK of *foreign-owned firms*. Some are of long standing (Singer, Fords): but many are not — and where most were once American, now many are Japanese, or Western European.

- The parallel *internationalization of the banks* and of financial institutions generally; and the way in which financial markets are now 24 hour phenomena, linked to each other globally by complex computer systems.

- The emergence of a *new international division of labour*, with the shift of industrial production out of the old 'core' capitalist economies (including the UK) into newly industrializing countries in Asia and in parts of Latin America.

- The *shift in world trade*, from a preoccupation with the sale of manufactured goods into the non-industrialized world (the nineteenth century pattern in the main) to one of selling manufactured goods largely into the home markets of already industrialized countries: with the associated intensification of competition between large manufacturers for those rich markets.

No doubt that list could grow: but we already have enough points to make it worthwhile redrawing the model of the economy we used for most of this unit. Diagram 5, for example, might well be redrawn as Diagram 13, to show that many multinational firms now straddle national boundaries, that banking networks are equally international in scope, that trade treaties lock the UK into international economic systems, and that the whole economy is subject to fierce international competition and the international movement of labour.

Such a redrawing suggests two possible final thoughts for this unit.

1   Can governments in the 1990s rely any more on the policy options of the post-war period, when those policy-options seemed to assume a high degree of freedom of manoeuvre for the UK economy and state? Or can the capacity for economic management only be recaptured by governments acting collectively at the supra-national level (at say that of the European Community), managing a bloc of economies strong enough to resist some of these international forces?

Can you see those options in Diagram 13? If it is no longer possible to control the economy from within the big square because of the global forces corroding its boundaries, then it seems that either the boundaries need strengthening or the box needs enlarging. Strengthening the boundaries (with import controls and the like) would reduce the global forces at work within the economy – but of course at the enormous cost of reduced access to the world's goods and markets. Enlarging the square — fusing this economy with others to make a bigger regional economy — would pull lots of those global forces inside again, for management by some supra-national political body. The cost here might also be enormous, but it would be of a different kind — a loss of sovereignty by the UK state.

2   What consequence does all that we have read have for the power and sovereignty of democratically-elected governments in the UK? If economies are so hard to manage, and if their increasing integration into global patterns of production and exchange makes that management more difficult, where does that leave politics in the UK in the 1990s?

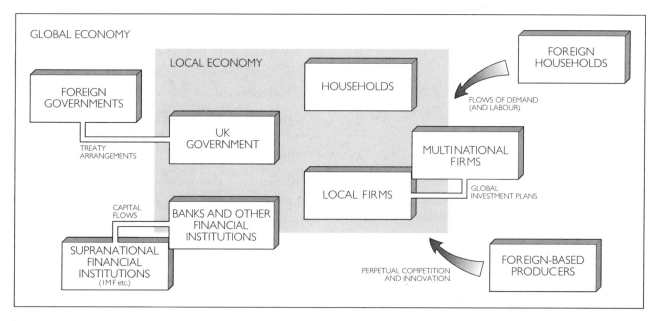

Diagram 13

These are questions which are easier to pose than to answer. But their presence in our minds should help to clarify much of the popular discussion of economic policy that now surrounds us. Their presence also prepares the way to the subject matter of the next block of this course — when we will examine in more detail questions of sovereignty, power and democracy.

REFERENCES

Alford, B. (1988) *British Economic Performance 1945–1975*, London, MacMillan.

Bootle, R.P. (1985) 'Monetary policy' in Morris, D. (ed.) *The Economic System in the UK*, Oxford, Oxford University Press.

Clarke, P. (1988) *The Keynesian Revolution in the making*, Oxford, Clarendon Press.

Coates, D. (1984) *The Context of British Politics*, London, Hutchinson.

Coates, D. and Hillard, J. (eds.) (1987) *The Economic Revival of Modern Britain: the debate between Left and Right,* Aldershot, Edward Elgar.

Hutchinson, T.W. (1968) *Economics and Economic Policy in Britain 1946–66*, London, Allen and Unwin.

Maynard, G. (1988) *The Economy under Mrs. Thatcher*, Oxford, Basil Blackwell.

Rowthorn, R.E. and Wells, J.R. (1987) *De-industrialization and Foreign Trade*, Cambridge, Cambridge University Press.

ACKNOWLEDGEMENTS

Grateful acknowledgement is made to the following sources for permission to reproduce material in this unit:

Text

Glyn, A. Ch.11 'A Million Jobs a Year', Minford, P. Ch.23 'Unemployment Cause and Cure', Smith, J. Ch.5 'An Industrial Strategy for Britain', and The Institute of Directors. Ch.18. 'Job Creation with a U-Turn' in Coates, D. and Hillard, J. (eds) *The Economic Revival of Modern Britain*, Edward Elgar Publishing Ltd., 1987.

Tables

Table 1: from Maynard, E. *The Economy under Mrs Thatcher*, Basil Blackwell, 1988.

UNIT 13   CONSTRUCTING MODELS

Prepared for the Course Team by Vivienne Brown

CONTENTS

I   INTRODUCTION

In this block we have been exploring aspects of the economy — how work is organized, how markets work, and how the aggregate economy works. Each of the units has looked at different aspects of the economy and has raised different questions about the economy. In this unit we shall see that, in spite of these differences in subject matter, there are also some important links and similarities. One point of similarity arises from a shared concern with the performance and productiveness of the economy, although the approach to this varies across the units. Another more methodological similarity arises from the units' shared concern to raise questions about the economy, and to discuss a range of possible answers. In doing this, each unit discusses a number of alternative economic models, and it is the different models that provide us with different answers. In this end-unit we shall be revising key economic issues in the block by reviewing this range of different economic models.

In addition, as you may remember from Unit 9, the end-units of the blocks together form a sequence which examines different aspects of social science thinking, gradually building up an overall picture of the 'cycle' of social science enquiry. In Unit 9 you looked at how concepts such as 'class' and 'gender' are used in the social sciences, and in doing so you considered why social scientists need concepts in order to try to understand society. But just as we need concepts in order to discuss issues in society, so we also need models to discuss the relationships involved in those issues. In this end-unit we shall build on the discussion of concepts in Unit 9 by examining models and model building in the social sciences. We shall find that much of that earlier discussion on concepts has a strong bearing on models and model building in the social sciences. This discussion will continue in Unit 18 which considers evidence and theories in the context of the concerns of Block IV.

I want in this unit to build on the dual character of concepts that you met in Section 5 of Unit 9. You saw there that conceptualization involves 'mental or linguistic representations of reality'. Concepts enable us to 'pick out' various features of the world and give them labels; this is the process of *representation*, in which concepts are our attempts to refer to or signify things going on in the world. But notice that this attempt to represent the real world necessarily takes place through language; our representations always have a *linguistic* dimension. Our attempt to represent the real world is thus part of the wider social process of using language to communicate with each other, and this is the process of *communication*. These two aspects — the representational and the communicative — are intertwined in a close and fascinating way, as you saw in Unit 9; it means that representation is always embedded in the wider social context of communication and language.

In this unit we shall see that these two aspects of conceptualization are also present in the models that we use to try to understand the economy: on the one hand, models provide a way of trying to understand the real economy; but on the other hand, we know that models are linguistic constructions expressed through shared forms of language and communication. Section 2 will discuss the 'representational' aspect of economic models, and Section 3 will consider the 'communicative' aspect of models. Section 4 will pull these two discussions together by examining what we can say about the relation between models and 'reality'. You will then be well placed to tackle the discussion in Unit 18, which considers the relation between facts and theories.

SUMMARY

- This end-unit will revise the key issues and economic models of Block III.

- In the course of doing so, it will also examine models and model building, drawing on the discussion of concepts in Unit 9.

2 REPRESENTATION AND THE ECONOMY

2.1 OBSERVING THE ECONOMY?

I have suggested that our need for models in trying to represent the economy is similar to our need for concepts, but here the question may well be raised again: why can't we simply go out and observe the economy? In Unit 9 it was argued that 'pure' observation or 'empiricism' is impossible; as you saw in the duck-rabbit and the staircase examples (Section 4), perception alone is not sufficient, even when we might think that we are observing something simple in a straightforward or objective way. Consider the enormous scale of the economy; where would we start if we wanted simply to observe it? Inevitably, if we set out to examine the economy or observe it in any way, we need to have a starting point of some sort, however rudimentary. This 'starting point' would be a kind of 'model'; it would be a view of the economy outlining the significant relationships that need further investigation.

For example, following on from the personal story of Jim Jarratt in Unit 10, we might decide to examine the causes of unemployment. To do this we would need a model of some sort: Unit 12 provided a *model of the aggregate economy* which placed unemployment in the wider context of economic processes such as investment, inflation, government economic policy, and international competition. In fact, in Unit 12 you met two such models of the aggregate economy — a Keynesian model and a monetarist model. These models give us an overall system or network of the significant economic relationships for understanding unemployment, its causes and its effects. Thus, *economic models help us to represent the economy as a system of economic relationships which enable us to identify (and sometimes to measure) the causes and effects of economic events.* How we do this depends to a certain extent on the questions that we are asking and the concepts and knowledge that we already have, but the basic function and role of the economic model remains the same.

In addition, the real economy is a very complex set of relations and so we need to *simplify* it before we can begin to understand it. We do this by picking out particular aspects or relationships for detailed analysis. You met this argument in Unit 4, Section 4, where it was argued that the process of 'abstraction' involves picking out particular aspects of society in isolation from the rest. Also, Unit 9 emphasized that the use of concepts helps us to generalize and simplify the variety and complexity of real phenomena; for example, it mentioned the concept 'dog' which helps us to generalize from a myriad array of individual canine quadrupeds. In the same way, economic models pick out a simpler version of the economy by focusing on one aspect of economic processes and ignoring others.

As an example, consider the flow diagrams that you met in Unit 12. These flow diagrams are used to represent the aggregate economy; the flow of money income and expenditure travels in one direction, while the opposite flow represents goods and services received in exchange. Here the aggregate economy is conceived as a series of money flows in one direction matched by an equal and opposite flow of goods and services (including labour services) in the other direction. This is itself a particular conception of the aggregate economy, and one which has been very influential. This idea of the aggregate economy is a very simple one (or it is when you get used to it!), compared with the many and varied economic deals and activities that we read about in the newspapers.

But this simple idea of flows of money payments and reciprocal flows of goods and services can be represented in various degrees of complexity. As the progression of diagrams in Unit 12 shows, the flow model of the aggregate economy can come in a number of different versions. It can be restricted to households and firms, as in Diagrams 1 and 2 in Unit 12, or it can be made more complex, as in Diagrams 3 to 6, where banks, government and the overseas sector are added. Although these diagrams may look different at first sight, the general underlying principle behind them all is the same. And the diagrams could be made even more complex still! For example, if we wanted to ask questions about the effect of changing unemployment on our model, we could divide the household sector into those households which include employed members and those which do not. From this we can see that models can vary in their degree of complexity and detail, even though they remain simple and abstract when compared with the myriad of activities in the real economy.

In this process of simplification we have to make a choice, and here we are guided by what we think is important. In this way, the process of simplification and of picking out the significant aspects already implies a judgment about what is important and what is worth investigating. Thus, while economic models pick out a simpler version of the economy for us, they also include a view of what is important and relevant. In Unit 10, for example, it was shown how the identification of paid labour with 'work' tends to make non-paid forms of work, such as housework, charitable work and voluntary work, slip from view and become 'invisible'.

Models also provide us with a way of organizing the *empirical evidence* of the actual economy. Without a model to guide us, we would not know what kind of economic data would be helpful. Referring back to Unit 10, if we think that the growth potential of the economy is affected by the sectoral composition of employment or output as between manufactures and services, or as between the marketed sector and the non-marketed sector, then we shall need empirical evidence on these different sectors to test our model. Alternatively, once the private domain has been identified as lying outside the 'economy', there is little incentive to collect statistics on it, and this then reinforces its invisibility. Or, returning to Unit 12, once we have settled on a Keynesian model of aggregate demand, we know exactly what kind of economic data we need. If the model says that it is aggregate demand that determines the level of unemployment and inflation, then we are going to need data on aggregate demand. This evidence is sought not only by economists but also by the government of the day anxious to keep track of the effects of its own economic policy, and by the financial and manufacturing sectors of the economy who need to be kept informed on the progress of the economy. In the UK, this kind of information is provided on a regular basis by the Central Statistical Office which publishes a number of official statistical publications, such as *Economic Trends*, which are available in most public and college reference libraries.

In the late 1980s, there was an increase in the rate of inflation and this was generally attributed to the increased level of domestic spending. During this period, the statistical data on consumers' expenditure and investment expenditure were watched extremely closely to monitor the effects of the government's policy of high interest rates, and so the official statistics on consumers' expenditure became headline news. It is easy to take these statistics for granted as an obvious way of measuring the real economy, but their collection and publication by the government (at some considerable expense) is the result of the power and pervasiveness of economic models of the aggregate economy which have helped to develop the concepts and categories of aggregate expenditure.

SUMMARY

- Economic models are needed because 'pure' observation of the real economy is impossible.

- Economic models pick out certain specified economic relationships from the myriad of economic activities in the real economy.

- Economic models are composed of a system or network of interlocking economic relationships which enable us to identify the causes and effects of economic events.

- Economic models may be more or less complex depending on the questions that are being asked, but they are simple compared with the complexity of the real economy.

- Economic models provide us with a way of identifying and organizing relevant empirical evidence.

2.2 ECONOMIC MODELS AND ECONOMIC CONCEPTS

In Unit 9 you learned about 'contested concepts', concepts whose meaning is not settled or agreed upon, but which have been subject to a range of competing definitions. This means that some social science concepts are subject to different meanings; concepts such as 'class' and 'capitalism', for example. In Unit 11, we examined the economic concept 'competition', and there too we found that different economists have attached different meanings to this term. For example, Schumpeter argues that competition involves a dynamic rivalry between firms that forces them to innovate, introducing new products and new processes. The concept of competition used in the neoclassical approach, however, is one that focuses on changes in price which secure an equilibrium between demand and supply in the case where there are very many firms. Thus, just as Unit 7, Part 1 and Unit 9 examined different meanings of 'class', so Unit 11's discussion showed that different meanings of 'competition' are being employed in discussions of the market. For this reason, we could say that 'competition' is an example of an essentially contested concept.

In Unit 11 we also saw that these different meanings of the concept 'competition' are used in different models of the market. Schumpeter's concept of dynamic competition over new goods was an integral part of his model of creative destruction where firms have to innovate or perish; and the neoclassical concept of equilibrium price was an integral part of the model of perfect competition where demand equals supply. In each case, we can see a close link between the concept of competition and the model of the market, but in each case the meaning of the concept 'competition' and the model of competition are different.

This illustrates the point you met in Unit 9, Section 6, that different models (or theories) employ or 'privilege' different key concepts. Looked at from this point of view, it can be helpful to think of a model (or theory) as a structured set of relationships between its key concepts; as we saw above, in the case of an economic model these economic relationships enable us to identify the causes and effects of economic events. In Unit 7, Part I, we saw that a model of 'class' postulates a set of relations between 'class' and the economy, property, economic power, income, status, political control, professional hierarchies, kinship groups, or whatever are the crucial concepts of that model; such a relationship may be that 'class is an important factor in causing or determining that person's life-chances'. In Unit 11, an economic model of the 'market' postulates a set of relationships between its own market concepts — concepts such as competition, price, costs, profits, capital, innovation, information, demand, supply, or whatever. Here such a relationship may be: 'equilibrium price is determined by demand and supply', or 'a firm's ability to survive and be profitable is determined by its ability to innovate ahead of rivals.'

In this course we use the terms 'theory' and 'model' interchangeably. However, different conventions in different social science disciplines can suggest different emphases between the term 'model' and the term 'theory'. Sometimes, 'model' is used for the more abstract or mathematical versions of a theory, and 'theory' is sometimes used for the more historically inclined or more open-ended versions of a model; but we won't be pursuing these distinctions in this course.

SUMMARY

- Some economic concepts may be contested; for example, 'competition'.
- Different economic models privilege different key concepts.
- In this course, the terms 'model' and 'theory' have more or less the same meaning.

CONCLUSION

In this section I have outlined some of the ways in which we use models to try to represent the real economy. Because we cannot simply observe the actual economy, we have to use models to carry out economic analysis. These models are composed of a system or network of economic relationships which specify the causes and effects of economic events. Economic models may be more or less complex, and always carry with them a particular view of what are the most significant economic relationships for further analysis.

3 THE LANGUAGE OF REPRESENTATION

3.1 METAPHORS OF MODEL CONSTRUCTION

So far in this end-unit I have concentrated on the representational aspect of economic models — that we use them to try to understand the real economy. But as you saw in Unit 9, conceptualization and model building are the outcome of a social process of enquiry about the world, and in this process we are using a shared language to communicate our views and persuade others. Because of this, the representational aspect of model building is always 'embedded' in this larger social frame of reference where language, forms of persuasion, and indeed the power of knowledge itself, become significant.

One way of appreciating this 'communicative' or 'linguistic' aspect of models is to notice the kind of language that we use when discussing models. For example, notice how often we talk about 'building' or 'constructing' a model. The language we are using here is the same as for building a house or something physical or material. But when social scientists 'build' models they are not building anything physical at all; they are thinking, writing and talking in a different way. In the process of doing so, they may well be constructing new concepts or adapting old ones, and they may well be thinking about these concepts in a new way; but when we use the words 'building' and 'constructing' in this context we are not referring to the physical activity of building or constructing, even though the activity may be very hard work.

We also freely use other terms connected with building and construction: we talk about providing 'solid foundations'; a good 'framework'; a theoretical 'edifice'; 'concrete' analysis; and we even refer to concepts as 'the building blocks' of analysis. Are we using these terms in a purely 'literal' sense where we mean exactly what we appear to be saying? Do we mean that concepts really *are* building blocks? Or are we using these terms in a *figurative* sense where we mean that concepts are *like* building blocks? Much of our language about models appears to be highly *metaphorical*, in that we appear to use language figuratively to discuss one thing in terms of something else; we talk about model building *as though* we were building a house.

I have just emphasized the language of building and construction, but there are other common metaphorical uses that seem to recur again and again. One common set of metaphors are *spatial metaphors* that rely on notions of space, distance, position and movement. How many times in the course have you read about the 'terrain' or 'domain' of a model, and having a map to help you find your way across unknown territory? How often do we refer to a theoretical 'position' and how often do we make a 'point' in demonstrating an argument? We even talk about coming 'straight to the point' in contrast with an argument that is 'all over the place'. We read of different 'levels' of analysis where we must probe 'beneath' the detail of our everyday lives or beneath the detail provided by empirical surveys, in order to discover the 'underlying' processes or the 'fundamental' reality. This notion of a vertically ordered intellectual space also corresponds with other ways of talking, when we say that something is 'deep' or 'profound', or that we want to get to the 'bottom' of something, or do 'in-depth' analysis.

In a number of ways, then, when we talk about models in the social sciences, our language seems to become permeated with metaphors. I have already referred to construction metaphors and spatial metaphors. *Visual metaphors*, too, abound when we try to talk about how we understand new concepts and models: we talk about the 'insights' that a model may give us; we talk about being 'blind' to new ideas, 'seeing' the light, or 'seeing eye to eye'; we 'focus' our attention here and 'see' a new 'perspective' there.

─────────────────── ACTIVITY 1 ───────────────────

We have seen how metaphors and figurative language seem to permeate our thinking.

As another example of how readily this happens, try describing a recent economic or political event. To what extent does your own account rely on this kind of language? Consider the liberalization of the City of London as the 'Big Bang', privatization as 'selling the family silver', and the economic 'cycle' as 'slump' and 'depression'.

───

> ### SUMMARY
>
> - Our thinking about social science models seems to be imbued with metaphorical language.
> - This metaphorical language seems to have a ready appeal and to make difficult or abstract ideas more accessible.

3.2   METAPHORS AND ECONOMIC MODELS

In Section 3.1 we saw that metaphorical ways of thinking seem to be important for model building. We can also see something of this at work in the liberal models of the market that were discussed in Unit 11. For each of these models, the writer quoted in the unit felt the need to present his account of the model in terms of a metaphor. I wonder if you noticed this at the time of reading the extracts quoted in Unit 11? Perhaps not; you may well have been so absorbed in making sense of the economics that you weren't aware of the metaphorical presentation of the argument. Perhaps the metaphors seemed 'right' in some way, so that you did not stop to think about them.

─────────────────── ACTIVITY 2 ───────────────────

This would be a good moment to return to the two liberal models of the competitive market outlined in Unit 11. Find the extracts which exemplify these models, and read them again. The extracts are:

- Schumpeter; Section 3.2 p.57.
- Arrow; Section 3.3 pp.63–4.

When you re-read these extracts, try to take note of the ways in which the authors express themselves using metaphors.

───

Schumpeter emphasizes that capitalism is a dynamic system that is constantly changing. His concept of competition as dynamic competition reinforces this as it is the never-ending competition between firms that provides the 'motor' for this dynamism. Did you notice that, at one point, Schumpeter refers to 'the capitalist engine'? This stresses the idea that capitalism is a system that is always in motion, always on the move, unleashing tremendous energy for transforming the world.

However, I think the main metaphor that drives this passage is not the mechanical metaphor of engines in motion, but a series of biological metaphors which emphasize the natural biological processes of growth and decay summarized in the phrase 'creative destruction'. In the first sentence, Schumpeter refers to capitalism as an 'evolutionary process' which is always changing and never stationary. What does this metaphor mean to you, I wonder? To me, it suggests the notion that change is an essential and integral part of capitalism; it is inconceivable that capitalism could stand still. It also suggests that this process of incessant change is itself 'natural', as biological changes might be thought 'natural'. In Unit 6 (and elsewhere) you considered the power of this notion that social processes are represented to us as natural in some way. Indeed, living at the end of the twentieth century we may well accept as entirely 'natural' the idea that we are living in a world of constant change, but historically this is a comparatively recent phenomenon. For most of human history, each generation has grown up in the secure knowledge that their lives would be pretty much the same as those of their parents and forebears.

Another thought that comes to me when reading about an 'evolutionary process' in the twentieth century is that we are all the product of 'evolution'; that all forms of life on this planet are the product of a spontaneous process where species thrive or decline according to their potential for adaptation to their environment. This suggests to me that the same kind of process is being implied here; that those people and those enterprises thrive most which readily adapt to social and economic change — survival of the fittest. Underlying all this, for me, there is also an implicit value judgement that all this change is beneficial and healthy: just as evolution in the biological world has produced intelligent and sentient life from the primordial slime, so capitalism is, overall, a story of social and economic progress and improvement.

Is this reading too much into a simple metaphor? The biological metaphor itself is clearly important to the author, for he returns to it again later in the passage when he refers to industrial change as industrial 'mutation', recognizing that this is a term borrowed from biology. Elsewhere in the book from which the extract is taken (Schumpeter, 1976), Schumpeter refers to capitalism as an 'organic' process, again reinforcing the notion that capitalism is a living force.

It is also worth noting a few general points about the author's use of biological metaphors in this passage. *First*, note how easily the author makes use of metaphorical language. Sometimes this is done quite unselfconsciously, as in the first sentence where Schumpeter states that capitalism is an evolutionary process; sometimes the author seems more aware of it, as when he refers to mutation as a biological term. *Second*, the author needs the metaphor to try to explain his own view of capitalism. In trying to say something that he feels is new or different, he needs to use metaphorical language to express his thoughts. Have you ever found yourself doing this? Struggling to say something, you come up with a figure of speech that just seems to sum up your own insight in a flash? *Third*, note how rich the interpretation of a metaphor can be. I wrote two whole paragraphs on just a couple of words written by Schumpeter, and I could have written more. But perhaps your own response to the biological metaphors was different from mine? Perhaps your own interpretation was different? This brings us to a *fourth point* worth noting. Part of the power of figurative language lies in its openness — more so than for language generally (though this itself is worth thinking about). This means that there isn't just one unique way of understanding it; it can reach out to different people in different ways.

The second model of the market explained in Unit 11 was the neoclassical model, and the relevant excerpt, by Kenneth Arrow, is in Section 3.3 of that unit. How did you get on with this one? As I read this passage, it was the metaphor of balance and equilibrium that struck me, and indeed this has been a very powerful metaphor in economics. It provides a very graphic illustration of the way in which price changes can result in an equality of demand and supply, where the quantity demanded equals the quantity supplied. It was partly for this reason that I decided in Unit 11 to illustrate the demand and supply model using a diagram of a pair of weighing scales, although this type of diagram is not used in conventional economics textbooks. (The conventional approach is to use a demand and supply diagram. This is the method used in the Second Level Economics Course: D216: *Economics and Changing Economies*.)

This metaphor helps to deepen our understanding. By seeing the operation of the market as an equilibrating mechanism where changes in price restore equality between demand and supply, we are given new insights and we are led to ask new questions about its operation. For example, in keeping with the metaphor of balance, we might want to ask by how much demand or supply would have to change in order to restore equilibrium; this question might well be suggested by the notion of a balance between two items, such as we saw in Figures 1–3 in Unit 11. Or we might be led to ask questions about the *stability* of such an equilibrium; for example, if there is a small movement away from the equilibrium position, is it possible for a new equilibrium to be established? Historically, the connections between economics and physics have helped to stimulate the use of mathematics in constructing economic models. This interest in mathematical models has grown enormously during the twentieth century and has shaped the modern development of economics as a discipline.

But as we saw with Schumpeter's biological metaphor, the particular effect of any metaphor will depend on the way it is constructed. Our understanding of the model is not simply 'deepened' but is given momentum in a specific direction. And what is this direction in the case of the metaphor of balance? Equilibrium is essentially a static concept; an economy in equilibrium is an economy where all economic variables are in a state of rest. In addition, in the neoclassical model of perfect competition, demand and supply are equal at the equilibrium price. This emphasis on equilibrium has arguably directed attention towards static analysis rather than dynamic analysis; as we saw in Unit 11, change is analysed as a comparison of equilibrium outcomes rather than as a continuous process of change and adaptation to new conditions.

Metaphors thus help to move a model in a specific direction. But as we saw in the case of Schumpeter, they may have other effects too. The metaphor of balance and equilibrium has been a powerful one for economics, and some of this power may well derive from its reference to physics and mathematics. This could work in two related ways.

First, the metaphor works by associating economics, which studies the laws of the market, with physics which studies the laws of the universe. Given the intellectual prestige of physics and its undeniably scientific status, the effect here is that some of the scientific status of physics rubs off on to economics. Indeed, one of the ways in which metaphors work is through the reader making an association between the unlike things being compared; without this background knowledge the metaphor would be meaningless. I therefore suspect that the ease or discomfort with which you responded to the balancing diagrams in Unit 11 has a lot to do with how you see yourself in relation to the mechanical world, or to an early school experience of physics — something perhaps which you hadn't thought much about before now. If the world of physics seems distant and unapproachable to you, then you might have been put off by the diagrams. If, on the other hand, you feel at home with mechanical analogies or have had experience of weights and weighing, then the diagrams would probably have been very straightforward (even too simple?) for you. But in the wider community, the conventional view of physics is that it is an eminently respectable scientific subject which has enormously increased our understanding of the physical world. Thus, a metaphor that associates physics with economics, the newer and less certain discipline, is one whose effect is to enhance the standing of economics.

The second way in which the metaphor of balance works by drawing on the natural sciences is by suggesting a similarity between the objects of the natural world and the objects of the economy. Just as the relative weight of two items is something determined within the natural world by the laws of mechanics, so (the inference surely is) the balancing of demand and supply and the determination of the equilibrium price that assures this balancing is also something beyond the powers of human agency to modify. The laws of demand and supply therefore become doubly associated with the laws of physics: not only do the laws of demand and supply have something of the status and the certainty of the laws of physics and mathematics, but they are also laws that are given and immutable and so not susceptible to reform or adaptation.

Here again we come across the distinction between the social and the natural. As you have seen at a number of points in the course, in debates about society and the economy there is an ongoing discussion about the relative spheres of the natural and the social, the ways in which they overlap, and the ways in which our perceptions of both the natural and the social world are subject to construction and reconstruction. In a basic discussion of the operation of the market, a similar set of issues has arisen: to what extent can the operation of the market be conceived of as 'natural' and therefore something we must simply submit to, and to what extent is it a 'social' process subject to social determinations and amenable to forms of social control? But in the case of the market, we see that this issue, this debate between the natural and the social, is already inscribed in the language that we use. The very language of the market is therefore not neutral as between opposing views of its operation, as the vocabulary we use to talk through its effects is one whose figurative resonances seem to lend support to one side of the debate.

SUMMARY

- Models themselves are often presented metaphorically; for example, markets are an evolutionary process, or a balancing of demand and supply.
- Our response to these models is partly affected by our response to these metaphors.

CONCLUSION

In this section, I have looked at some of the ways in which metaphors are used in discussing social science models and in formulating models of the economy. These metaphorical usages have a ready intuitive appeal and can often be organized around familiar objects or ideas in a way that makes abstract ideas and arguments more intelligible to us. This emphasis on metaphor reinforces the point that representation and analysis of the real economy have a linguistic and communicative aspect, and are therefore embedded in the wider social context of language and persuasion.

4   MODELS AND REALITY

Economic concepts and models help us to understand the economy. But as we have seen, this process of representation is inseparable from the activity of constructing models and trying to persuade others. Our knowledge is conceptually mediated, and in this sense concepts and models are always social constructions, no matter how much they seem to be giving us straight descriptions of reality.

As an example of this, consider again the aggregate demand model we were examining in Section 2. In Unit 12, this model was presented in a number of different ways. It was presented using flow diagrams as we saw above, and it was also presented in words by saying that aggregate demand is equal to the sum of consumers' expenditure, investment expenditure, government expenditure, and net exports. Yet another account of this model was provided in Section 4.1 in Unit 12 where it was written in symbols instead of words:

Aggregate Demand $= c + i + g + x - m$

We see then that Unit 12 provided a number of different ways of thinking about the components of aggregate expenditure. But did you respond to them all in the same way I wonder? What difference does it make to your understanding or intuitive feel for the model, whether you think of aggregate expenditure as a set of payments between different economic agents, or as a series of symbols, or as a circular flow diagram?

 ACTIVITY 3

Try thinking about this question. What were your responses to these different representations of the model of aggregate expenditure? Why do you think you did respond in these ways?

I wonder how you answered this activity. My guess would be that most people would feel most at ease with the circular flow diagram — well, the simpler versions anyway! — and would be least at ease with the symbols, which can seem rather formal and abstract, even though they are just ordinary letters of the alphabet. If this was the case for you, then it is not surprising that it was also the case for many other students as well. And I think there is a general point here: how a model is actually presented to us, how a course unit is actually written in terms of the style and sound of the voice within the text, will affect our response to that model or that unit.

In the same way, how models are presented within the academic environment affects their popularity or success in influencing further thinking or research in particular areas. There are examples, for instance, of economic models being overlooked or rejected in their own time but then rediscovered as brilliant contributions to knowledge by later generations of economists. In economics, for example, many early mathematical models were simply incomprehensible at the time. This reminds us not only that the *construction* of models is influenced by wider social factors, but also that the *reception* and the *interpretation* of models is affected by institutional factors within the academic community.

We have just seen that we are influenced by the way that a particular model is presented to us. Furthermore, once we have set up our model of aggregate expenditure in a particular way, we find that it is difficult simply to lay aside the particular access or insights that this formulation has seemed to give us. For example, once aggregate demand has been presented as a circular flow of expenditures repeating itself continuously over time, this seems to say something about the economy which is not captured by writing down a row of letters or even by writing in full the names of the component expenditures.

This means that the kinds of questions we are prompted to ask about the economy are going to be influenced to some extent by the representation of the model. We are led to ask questions such as — Does the circle grow larger over time? Are there breaks in the circle (leakages from the flow)? Does the circle become a spiral? What are the conditions for the process to become a vicious circle of economic decline or a virtuous circle of economic growth? (Is it a merry-go-round of money making or is it the heavenly orbit of the planets?) In this way we see that the metaphor hasn't only provided an intuitive feel for the theory. It has also perhaps given us insights about the economy that might otherwise have been unavailable to us; by this I mean that our understanding of the real economy itself may well have been changed by the presentation of the model as a circular flow diagram.

What this example shows, I think, is that the process of representation never sets out from a blank piece of paper or a blank mind; we have to try to interpret the world in ways that make sense to us now. And in attempting to interpret what we don't yet know, we necessarily draw upon the stock of meanings that are already familiar to us. By applying and extending the meanings of the familiar world, we often use them figuratively to help make sense of the less familiar. Thus, the activity of model building is sometimes compared to the construction of new metaphors that reveal new relationships.

This awareness of the linguistic and cultural dimensions of knowledge and representation underlines the point that knowledge is conceptually and socially constructed. It also cautions us against assuming too readily or too easily that our models are a 'true' representation of the real economy. Absolute terms such as the 'real' and the 'true' are very powerful; of course we try to teach children how to tell the truth, but it is only in straightforward cases that we can have confidence that our knowledge is securely based. Appeals and counter-appeals to the 'truth' may have a high-sounding ring to them, but in practice we have to go beyond this to examine carefully and in detail the specific forms of argument and evidence in each case. Very often, as a result of this sort of critical investigation, we have to be rather sceptical of the claims made by the proponents of a particular model. The model may well give us insights and deepen our understanding, but it is not likely to be the whole story. There may well be other aspects of the issue that are not so well captured by that model, or there may still be unanswered questions that need further examination.

For this reason, although we rely on models for providing us with analytical concepts and for pointing out the way for empirical investigation, we may hesitate before declaring that they are true or false in themselves. Economic models, for instance, help us to understand how the economy works, but we don't believe that any model has spoken the last word. As an example of this kind of scepticism, consider this careful assessment of a full version of the neoclassical model: 'The ... model is essentially a generalization, to the entire economy and to all markets simultaneously, of the ancient and elementary notion that prices move to levels which equilibrate demand and supply. No intellectual construction of this scope, designed to address basic questions in a subject as complex and elusive as economics, can be described as simply true or false ... ' (Scarf, 1987, vol.1, p.556). None the less, Scarf goes on to say that: 'In spite of its many shortcomings, the ... model — if used with tact and circum-spection — is an important conceptual framework for evaluating the conse-quences of changes in economic policy or in the environment in which the economy finds itself.' The attractions of this model of competitive equilibrium, then, are not that it is 'true' or that it describes the real economy in any direct or straightforward sense, but that it provides a conceptual framework for analysing real economic issues.

This view was also expressed by an economist reviewing Arrow's contribution to economics. The reviewer argued that Arrow's work was proof that: 'an abstract, non-descriptive theory has a powerful role to play in the serious analysis of actual economies. It provides, as it were, a way into the complexities and forces one to ask the right questions' (Hahn, 1986, p.333). This writer also argued that such a theory 'powerfully organizes thought without on its own being descriptive or conclusive' (ibid., p.334). The criteria presented here, then, for a good model are not that it is true, or describes reality, or answers all questions conclusively. The criteria are that it 'powerfully organizes thought' and forces one to ask the 'right questions'.

These quotations show that some economists do not necessarily judge the usefulness of a model by how well it represents economic reality in a direct and one-to-one way. Rather, they assess a model in more open-ended terms: it provides a structured framework for analysing the economy; it helps to organ-ize thought in a difficult area; it helps us to ask the right questions about the economy; it provides a way of thinking through the complexity of the real economy; it provides a way of sorting out relevant from irrelevant issues; and it is felt by its practitioners that the model has worked well in the past in contributing to analyses of real economic issues and economic problems.

But note that this open-ended recommendation for a model inevitably leaves open some important questions. When is thought being powerfully organized, as opposed to trivially organized? How can we know that we are asking the right questions about the economy? Where do these criteria for powerful thought and right answers come from? If these criteria have meaning in terms of the frame of reference of that particular model itself, how can this help us to decide between models? The issue of comparing models and choosing between them is the subject of Unit 26. The point I wish to make here is that the usefulness of models in explaining the real economy does not always hinge on their immediate correspondence with reality. It is argued, for example, that the competitive model of demand and supply gives us many insights into the working of the economy, even though equilibrium does not exist literally in the real economy. Similarly, marxists argue that capitalism is driven by the funda-mental antagonisms between capital and labour, even though they know that there are many people who don't fit easily into their definition of either the capitalist class or the working class.

Sometimes too the usefulness of a model is a rather pragmatic affair — whether the model opens up questions about the real world that seem important and interesting to its practitioners at that particular moment; whether it facilitates further empirical investigations; or whether it produces significant policy implications. This means that the historical and economic circumstances may also affect the extent of a model's influence, as they may also provide real-world 'tests' of that model's viability. For example, the monetarist criticisms of Keynesianism came to a head when Keynesianism seemed to be performing less well in the wake of the oil price shocks during the 1970s. And monetarism's own influence declined during the 1980s as the UK government's attempts to control, even to define, the money supply seemed beset with problems.

SUMMARY

- Models help us to understand reality but are themselves constructed within a social context of language and communication.
- The language or figurative elements of a model may affect our understanding of reality.
- It is often meaningless to ask whether a model itself is true or false.
- Social and institutional aspects of research and academic life may also affect the popularity, influence, or even the intelligibility of a model.

CONCLUSION

Economic models are powerful aids in helping us to understand the real economy; indeed, economists couldn't work without them. But we have also seen that economic models are intellectual constructions embedded in the social context of language and communication. Thus, we have seen that the dual character of models is such that, although they seem to be describing reality as it really is, we cannot simply view them as a 'replication' or 'mirror' of the real world. In some philosophical discussions (as you saw in Unit 9) this dual character has given rise to a debate between those who wish to emphasize the one aspect at the expense of the other. This has resulted in endless debates between the 'realists' and the 'relativists', as they are sometimes known: over the extent to which we can really know whether a model can give us insights into 'reality' when that reality is unknown to us except through the use of models of one sort or another; and over the extent to which models themselves can actually 'construct' our views of what reality is. At this stage in your studies it is probably most helpful to keep in mind the advice offered in Unit 9, and to see models as having a dual character combining both aspects, bearing in mind that there are different kinds of models, and that some may seem to take on one character more than the other.

5   CONSTRUCTING MODELS: CONCLUSION

I hope you can now see that model building is an essential part of studying the economy, and that there are sometimes a number of different models that can be drawn on when studying any particular aspect of the economy. Referring back to the first paragraph of this unit, a strong link between the units of Block

III, however different their subjects may appear to be, is that each tries to give a range of possible answers to economic questions. The range of possible answers arises from the discussion of different models within the units. This unit has tried to make those discussions more meaningful by stepping back and considering what is involved when we construct economic models.

In the course of this unit I have considered how the 'representational' and the 'communicative' aspects of economic models are closely intertwined. We use models to try to understand the real economy but at the same time we are aware that these models are themselves intellectual constructions, depending on the linguistic, analytical and even economic resources of the society. We noted that metaphorical ways of thinking seem to enter into our thought-processes at a very deep level, and seem to be particularly necessary and productive whenever we are grappling with difficult, strange, or new ideas. This insight might help us to recognize the similarities between many forms of intellectual endeavour, no matter how different they may appear at first sight in content or coverage. If both 'metaphor and model-making reveal new relationships' (Black, 1962, p.238), then we might see the affinities between work in the social sciences, the humanities and the physical sciences.

REFERENCES

Black, M. (1962) *Models and Metaphors,* Ithaca, NY, Cornell University Press.

Hahn, F. (1986) 'Living with uncertainties in economics', review of Arrow, K. *Collected Papers,* 6 vols, *Times Literary Supplement,* 1 August, pp.333–4.

Scarf, H.E. (1987) 'Computation of general equilibria', in Eatwell, J. et al. (eds) *The New Palgrave: A Dictionary of Economics*, London and Basingstoke, Macmillan.

Schumpeter, J.A. (1976) *Capitalism, Socialism and Democracy*, London, Allen & Unwin (first published in Britain in 1943).

FURTHER READING FOR BLOCK III

UNIT 10

Coote, A. and Campbell, B. (1982) *Sweet Freedom : The Struggle for Women's Liberation*, London, Pan Books.

Deane, P. and Cole, W.A. (1967) *British Economic Growth 1688–1959*, Cambridge, Cambridge University Press.

UNIT 11

Donaldson, P. and Farquhar, J. (1988) *Understanding the British Economy*, Harmondsworth, Penguin Books.

UNIT 12

Clarke, P. (1988) *The Keynesian Revolution in the Making*, Oxford, Oxford University Press.

Morris, D. (ed.) (1985) *The Economic System in the UK*, Oxford, Oxford University Press.